The Evolution of Strategic Thought Since September 11, 2001:
A Swiss Perspective on Clausewitz, Classical and Contemporary Theories

Grégoire Monnet

The Evolution of Strategic Thought Since September 11, 2001: A Swiss Perspective on Clausewitz, Classical and Contemporary Theories

Grégoire Monnet

2016
Carola Hartmann Miles-Verlag

CIP-Kurztitelaufnahme der Deutschen Nationalbibliothek:
Grégoire Monnet, The Evolution of Strategic Thought since September 11, 2001: A Swiss Perspective on Clausewitz, classical and contemporary Theories, Berlin 2016.

ISBN 978-3-945861-29-5

© Carola Hartmann Miles-Verlag,
(www.miles-verlag.jimdo.com;
email: miles-verlag@t-online.de)
Herstellung: Books on Demand GmbH, Norderstedt

Titelbild: Miles-Verlag/Scheiblich
Alle Rechte, insbesondere das Recht der Vervielfältigung und Verbreitung sowie der Übersetzung, vorbehalten. Kein Teil des Werkes darf in irgendeiner Form (durch Fotokopie, Mikrofilm oder ein anderes Verfahren) ohne schriftliche Genehmigung des Verlages reproduziert oder unter Verwendung elektronischer Systeme gespeichert, verarbeitet, vervielfältigt oder verbreitet werden.

Printed in Germany

TABLE OF CONTENT

I.	**INTRODUCTION**		15
	A.	MAJOR RESEARCH QUESTION	16
	B.	CLAUSEWITZ VERSUS JOMINI, YESTERDAY AND TODAY	16
	C.	POTENTIAL EXPLANATIONS AND HYPOTESIS	17
	D.	LIMITATIONS	19
	E.	LITERATURE REVIEW	20
		1. From 1989 to 2001	20
		2. On Counterinsurgency	23
		a. The Role of Chance	24
		b. The Role of Reason	25
		c. Hatred	25
	F.	RESEARCH DESIGN	27
II.	**CLAUSEWITZ'S INFLUENCE IN THE UNITED STATES BEFORE 2001**		29
	A.	CLAUSEWITZ IN THE U.S. MILITARY	30
		1. Clausewitz and the Generals	32
		2. Clausewitz and the Services	34
	B.	CLAUSEWITZ AND U.S. READERS	36
	C.	CLAUSEWITZ IN U.S. POLICY AND STRATEGY	40
	D.	CLAUSEWITZ'S CRITICS	43
	E.	CONCLUSION	45
III.	**CLAUSEWITZ'S INFLUENCE IN EUROPE: THE ORACLE OF NATO**		47
	A.	THE LONG ROAD TO NATO	47
	B.	PREPARATION FOR DEFENSE (1949–1989)	49

	C.	NATO'S USE OF FORCE (1991–2010)	57
	D.	CONCLUSION	61
IV.		**EFFECTS AND CONSEQUENCES OF CLAUSEWITZ ON COUNTERINSURGENCY**	63
	A.	SHIFTS IN THE TERRORIST REALM	63
	B.	THE LINKAGE BETWEEN TODAY TERRORISM AND THE TRINITY	64
	C.	A POSSIBLE TRINITARIAN APPROACH TO INSURGENCY	67
V.		**OLD NEW WARS AND THE ENDURING RELEVANCE OF CLAUSEWITZ**	78
	A.	ON THE NATURE OF WAR	78
	B.	CLAUSEWITZ'S TRINITY IN ACTUAL WAR WITH NON-STATE ACTORS	92
	C.	THE MISUSE AND MISINTERPRETATION OF "STRATEGY"	98
	D.	PURPOSE AND MEANS OF WAR	106
	E.	INSURGENCY: A PIVOT BETWEEN ESCALATION AND DE-ESCALATION	111
	F.	THE RELATIONSHIP BETWEEN OFFENSE AND DEFENSE IN STRATEGY	114
	G.	A WAR PLAN DESIGNED FOR THE TOTAL DEFEAT OF THE ENEMY	134
VI.		**CONCLUSION**	138
VII.		**LIST OF REFERENCES**	143

LIST OF FIGURES

Figure 1.	Clausewitz vs. Jomini in the English-Speaking World	37
Figure 2.	Clausewitz vs. Jomini in German-Speaking World	40
Figure 3.	Basic Trinity of an Involved Party	66
Figure 4.	Trinities' Interrelationship	66
Figure 5.	Winning "Hearts and Minds"	667
Figure 6.	Population Support Model	667
Figure 7.	Relationship Between Two Trinities	95
Figure 8.	Break-down of Trinities	96
Figure 9.	Assignment of Trinities within a Coalition	97
Figure 10.	Interactivity of Strategy and Policy into the Realm of Diplomacy and Politic	100
Figure 11.	Continuum of Violence	112

LIST OF TABLES

Table 1.	Trinity Interpretation	93
Table 2.	Clausewitz's Conditions for Effectiveness of a General Uprising	128

ABSTRACT

Since 1991, a long list of scholars has sought to write off Clausewitz as outdated and no longer worth study. In light of the past fifteen years and the absence of a strategic victory in the wars in Iraq and Afghanistan, however, Clausewitz's early retirement is misguided, to say the least. Are the classical theories of Clausewitz on the nature of war—particularly concerning small wars and insurgencies—relevant to contemporary conflicts since September 11, 2001?

This study is chiefly based on secondary sources, including books and scholarly articles originating from the work of scholars, political researchers, and think tanks. The research method is qualitative, and it compares, contrasts, summarizes, and critically assesses the adaptations of, and effects on, counterinsurgency policy, strategy, and doctrine in English-speaking nations and Europe.

The study shows that the content of Clausewitz's *On War* must be understood in the political and strategic context of the 21st century and not that of the 19th century. Now is the time to put aside visceral reactions against Clausewitz and start to study his work with closer attention, especially at the junction of the military and the political.

LIST OF ACRONYMS AND ABBREVIATIONS

CENTCOM	Central Command
CIA	Central Intelligence Agency
CinC	Commander in Chief
Col	Colonel
COIN	Counterinsurgency
CT	Counter-Terrorism
DC	Defence Committee (NATO)
DIME	Diplomatic, Informational, Military, and Economic
DOD	Department of Defense
EBAO	Effects-Based Approach Operation
ETA	Euskadi Ta Askatasuna
FDR	Franklin Delano Roosevelt
FM	Field Manual
GWOT	Global War on Terror
HQ	High Quarter
IRA	Irish Republican Army
ISIS	Islamic State of Iraq and Syria
JCS	Joint Chief of Staff
JPME	Joint Program for Military Education
LTC	Lieutenant Colonel
MC	Military Council (NATO)
NAC	North Atlantic Council
NATO	North Atlantic Treaty Organization
NVA	North Vietnamese Army
OODA	Boyd's Loop (Observe, Orient, Decide, Act)
PMESII	Politic, Military, Economic, Society, Informational, Infrastructures
RMA	Revolution in Military Affairs
SACEUR	Supreme Allied Command Europe
SASE	Safe and Secure Environment
SC	Strategic Concept (NATO)

SecDef	Secretary of Defense
STANAG	Standard Agreement (NATO)
SWAT	Special Weapons Attack Team
TRIPLE	Territory, Religion & Ideology, Identity, Political Arrangement, Language and Communication, Economics
UCK *Kosovës)*	Kosovo Liberation Army (*Ushtria Çlirimtare e*
UN	United Nations
UNSC	United Nations Security Council
USMA	United States Military Academy
USSR	Union of Soviet Socialist Republics
WWI	World War I
WWII	World War II

ACKNOWLEDGMENTS

I would like to acknowledge the following people without who, this book could not have been possible:

My parents, who gave to me two remarkable gifts that became handy at the Naval Postgraduate School: the passion for self-education and a passion for books.

Colonel GS Michael "Mike" Hächler, my former commander and mentor, at the Swiss NBC Defense Center, who gave me the opportunity to be posted at the Naval Postgraduate School and the honor to study with such high-quality and experienced professors and fellow students—most of whom became true friends during my year and a half of studies.

My thesis professors at NPS: Professor Donald Abenheim for his outstanding devotion, mentoring, and patience, enduring many drafts and discussions—without his unconditional help, this book would not have been what it is; Professor James Russel and Professor Carolyn Halladay for their help and contributions to this book; Professor Donald J. Stoker for his encouragement and help in finding documents to enlarge my understanding of Clausewitz; and Professors Daniel Moran and David Yost, who let me use craft seminar papers on the topic of my thesis. I also want to thank those scholars who took the time to answer my emails so that I better understood their works: Professor Christopher Bassford, Professor Tommas X. Hammes, and U.S. General David Petraeus (Ret).

Many friends who directly or indirectly supported me in my endeavor and especially U.S. Navy LCDR Waren Yu (Ret) for his friendly support and Dr. Cheryldee Huddleston, who, I hope, will not develop Clausewitz-related PTSD after so many revisions of this work.

Last but not least, my family. We had our first opportunity in thirteen years to spend a year and a half living together each day. However, they sacrificed some quality time to let me study in quietness. I can never thank them enough for that, especially Heather, my wonderful wife, who supported me despite my changes of moods during my coursework. Thank you to Ryan, my son, who was pleased to compare his better school grades to mine and was always optimistic about my capacity to learn and hopefully to one day reach his level. And finally, Meghan, my little Sunshine, who always makes my day with her smiles, even after exhausting and frustrating days of failed attempts to write the "right thing in the right spot."

I. INTRODUCTION

At the end of the Cold War, the regular armed forces of the Western world stumbled into an existential crisis because the Warsaw Pact, the main adversary on which they focused for almost five decades, vanished overnight without a fight. This existential crisis began with the fall of the Berlin Wall in 1989 and became a reality in 1991, with the dissolution of the Soviet Union and with the advent of war in south Eastern Europe and the Middle East.

In 1991, *The Transformation of War*[1] by Martin van Creveld appeared, the first influential mainstream text or manifesto criticizing Clausewitz. Published during the Gulf War, his book was a direct result of Israel's struggle, since 1948, with irregular conflict. From this vantage, van Creveld rejected what he deemed to be Carl von Clausewitz's theories as having little relevance in the face of terrorism, irregular war, and counterinsurgency as they manifested themselves with growing ferocity in the years after 1991.

His book influenced military thinkers for almost two decades as conflict in this period diverged from the Cold War's collective military memory of wide-scale combat and operational doctrine, especially after the second Iraqi campaign (2003) became bogged down in an insurgency. Van Creveld's approach resulted in two main consequences for makers of western strategy: Counterinsurgency began to be seen as a new and separate kind of war, and the military realm became even further separated from the political, resulting in a series of blunders at a strategic level.

Since nation-states have not disintegrated in the face of terrorism and irregular war, and because war in whatever form serves some political purpose, however diffuse, Clausewitz still plays a role in the analysis of war, especially from a continental European point of view. Technology may have evolved and influenced tactical approaches to operations and fighting, but the cornerstones of strategy have changed little since the inception of nuclear weapons in the middle 1940s.

---

[1] Published by The Free Press.

A scholar of enduring vision and importance for this age as well as his own, Bernard Brodie recognized that strategy under the nuclear threat changed the paradigm of a winnable war; henceforth, armed forces' first efforts were to avoid war through successful deterrence.[2] The end of the Cold War, as well as progress in the ballistic accuracy, command and control, targeting, and types of munitions, however, shifted this paradigm back to the possibility for armed forces to fight and win smaller wars, as had been imperative during Clausewitz's time.

A. MAJOR RESEARCH QUESTION

This volume wrestles with the following question: Are the classical theories of Carl von Clausewitz on the nature of war relevant since September 11, 2001, particularly concerning small wars and insurgencies? Second, this volume analyzes how and why such classical theory has played a role, whether positively or negatively in the 21st century. This volume strives to be of use to students of war as well as senior defense and military figures confronted with the perpetually changing face of contemporary military conflicts.

B. CLAUSEWITZ VERSUS JOMINI, YESTERDAY AND TODAY

The operational level of war is a recurrent friction point between the respective views of Clausewitz's and Jomini's schools of thought about the levels of war and the nature of war. The Jominian approach to war as science and the emphasis on the massing of overwhelming force at the decisive point through the able hands of a single, senior commander does not answer the need for comprehensive strategy, as Clausewitz has argued, because military might alone does not solve politically rooted problems.

Clausewitz, on the other hand, assumed that strategy not only must be defined before entering a war to create the desired political and strategic outcome, but these aspects can change constantly due to

---

[2] Lawrence Freedman, *Strategy: A History* (New York: Oxford University Press, 2013), 148–149.

the interaction and friction of war. He most famously noted that strategy is formed by the close intercourse of politics and military interaction. Thus, the armed forces adapt their tactics and operational plans if the strategy changes.

Winning a war is more than winning all battles; the political and strategic outcome should be better than at the start, and the result should be a safe and secure environment. In recent conflicts, from the ex-Yugoslav and Kuwait wars in the early 1990s onward, armed forces won all the battles, such as they were, but, especially in the cases of Iraq, Afghanistan, and Libya, the environments after the fighting subsided were neither safer nor secure. The political results have left much to be desired.

Hence, part of the problem may be situated at this juncture: the operational level in its classical character as delineated by Field Marshal Helmut von Moltke in the 19th century and as it has reemerged in 20th century conflicts. Today, at this level, the military interacts with the political in the wider sense of mass politics and the uses of violence.

Clausewitz's analytical work, *On War*, if carefully studied and properly used by students of war, may be the cornerstone of a comprehensive approach to counterinsurgency and future conflicts, despite the assertions of its many critics in the English-speaking world since September 11, 2001, and earlier. Far from being obsolete, Clausewitz remains one of the salient ways to understand the dynamics and greater truths of war and warfare.

C. POTENTIAL EXPLANATIONS AND HYPOTESIS

Clausewitz's work, *On War,* is an introspection on the relation between war and policy and on the nature of war in theory and war in fact. Specifically, Clausewitz linked fundamental principles between the two realms—policy and the political on the one hand, and, on the other, the military as it moved from its dynastic foundation to its national character—and their interactions. Clausewitz did not try to give a template for success; rather, he proposed a construct to conceptualize a comprehensive approach to maximize chances of success. This approach makes his work more relevant today than Jomini's "recipe," which, according to Jomini, should always bring success if executed correctly.

The U.S. armed forces have relied heavily on Jomini's work in their military training and education since the early 19th century. This reliance on Jomini has been the factor that has enabled the U.S. armed forces, throughout history, to formulate doctrine and to win battles amid successful campaigns in certain theaters of war. However, since World War II—for reasons that bear close examination today—U.S. forces are less successful in winning the peace once "Phase III" is completed.[3]

This record may be explained by the fact that Clausewitz is seldom read or understood by military or political leaders. The omission has important ramifications. The neo-Clausewitzian British officer and scholar Emile Simpson stated correctly that "Jomini ... writes about warfare rather than war. Clausewitz, on the other contrary, writes to explain war, shaped by society and politics, as it functions according to means and ends."[4]

Evidence of this dichotomy can be found in the military results in the recent conflicts in Afghanistan and Iraq, at the end of "Phase III" and the beginning of "Phase IV" until the withdrawal of the coalition troops. Observers of these wars saw the surprising presence of non-comprehensive approaches; it was a mistake to use the tactics of counterinsurgency as the grand strategy. The misreading of Clausewitz's "trinity" and the non-acceptance of counterinsurgency as

---

[3] U.S. Joint Chiefs of Staff, *Joint Operation Planning* (Washington, DC: Joint Chiefs of Staff, 2011), xxiii–xxiv. A military operation is sequenced in six phases: Phase 0 is the shaping; Phase I is the deterrence; Phase II is the seizure of initiative; Phase III is the domination; Phase IV is the stabilization; and Phase V is the enabling of the civilian authority. "Dominate (Phase III). The dominate phase focuses on breaking the enemy's will for organized resistance or, in noncombat situations, control of the operational environment. Stabilize (Phase IV). The stabilize phase is required when there is no fully functional, legitimate civil governing authority present. The joint force may be required to perform limited local governance, integrating the efforts of other supporting/ contributing multinational, IGO, NGO, or USG department and agency participants until legitimate local entities are functioning." Ibid.

[4] Emile Simpson, *War from the Ground Up: Twenty-First Century Combat as Politics* (New York: Oxford University Press, 2013), 136.

a part of the violence continuum[5] led planners to think about these conflicts with far too much optimism as a special case of warfare.

As a witness to war in its varied forms in the revolutionary and Napoleonic period, Clausewitz understood well what later came to be called counterinsurgency. This insight, however, is not recognized as such by his critics, and his theories are not applied correctly. The critics of Clausewitz read his theory with a (Jominian) didactic and tactically oriented approach. Therefore, they tend to misunderstand the relationship between the political and military realm at the strategic level during an operation. The vocabulary used by Clausewitz and Jomini is not adapted correctly in today's idiom, which has led to mistakes in the interpretation of their theories. This misinterpretation applies particularly to the word *strategy*, because before World War I, "strategy" was narrowly focused on military matters without regard for the diplomatic, informational, economic, or political realm of a country.

D. LIMITATIONS

This book grapples with the difficulties of having a comprehensive approach to the study of contemporary conflict that leads to a sound end. First, the way by which influences can be traced may be blurry or distorted. Second, the abundance of literature on Clausewitz and all interpretations of his work cannot be read in anything like their entirety to produce this book; the same can be said of the surfeit of information on recent conflicts.

Finally, part of this work is based on assumptions that are themselves based on literature and articles that rest on their own assumptions. Therefore, this book should be considered as a first step for a larger study or a doctoral dissertation. However, none of these limitations prevent a critical assessment of the literature used.

---

[5] Carl von Clausewitz, *On War*, ed. and trans. Michael Howard and Peter Paret (Princeton, NJ: Princeton University Press, 1984), 81. "Wars can have all degrees of importance and intensity, ranging from a war of extermination down to a simple armed observation."

E. LITERATURE REVIEW

The selected literature was reviewed in two steps—the first focusing more on Clausewitz's relevance prior to 9/11, and the second focusing more on Clausewitz in relation to insurgency.

1. From 1989 to 2001

According to both John Shy in *The Maker of Modern Strategy: From Machiavelli to the Nuclear Age*[6] and Bruno Colson in *La Culture Stratégique Américaine*,[7] the U.S. armed forces have throughout their history relied principally on Jomini for their education in strategy, that is, a prescriptive approach with its origins in the Napoleonic period and transmitted through American military doctrine. These doctrines of Jomini were injected into the education and training of the U.S. Army through West Point and the teachers of tactics and fortifications raised in the French school of military instruction of the mid-19th century.

Around the time of the U.S. defeat in Vietnam in 1975, a usable translation of Clausewitz was completed in the university world,[8] and his work started to be read more widely. In order to explain why Vietnam was unsuccessful, the armed forces turned their attention to Clausewitz and concluded that solutions in the military realm were not synchronized with the political realm.[9] The Goldwater-Nichols Act, which enabled the transformation of the armed forces structures in the mid-80s, is one of the reforms that grew from this intellectual shift.

Clausewitz's theories gained popularity during this period and were added to military academies' syllabi, but Clausewitz's contribution to a better understanding between the operational level and the strategic level had not reached its full potential. This fact is partially explained

---

[6] Peter Paret, Gordon Alexander Craig, and Felix Gilbert, *Makers of Modern Strategy: From Machiavelli to the Nuclear Age* (Princeton, NJ: Princeton University Press, 1986), 143–85.

[7] Bruno Colson, *La Culture Stratégique Américaine* (Paris: Economica, 1993).

[8] Michael Howard and Peter Paret edited a new translation in 1976 of *On War*. Carl von Clausewitz, *On War* (Princeton, NJ: Princeton University Press, 1984).

[9] Colson, *La Culture Stratégique Américaine*, 250.

by the victory of the first Gulf War (1991) where the success of the Jominian "AirLand Battle" concept again showed its validity,[10] and by the influence of van Creveld's *Transformation of War*.

During the same period, proponents of the Revolution in Military Affairs (RMA) were also joining to prove that Jomini's principles were even more relevant than before. The information revolution would help "the new weapons [to] ... make possible 'near-simultaneous operations' ... The emphasis would now be on speed, not mass."[11] The RMA improved efficiency at the tactical level and between the tactical and operational levels; however, it did not integrate it with the strategic-political decision-making process. Therefore, RMA is nothing more than what Clausewitz pointed out when he wrote, "Force ... equips itself with the inventions of art and science"[12] in order to contend against violence, an adaptation to new technologies, neither a revolution nor a new strategy.

The late 1980s, however, brought Jomini's and Clausewitz's theories closer in armed forces studies and doctrine. The First Gulf War demonstrated how, since Vietnam, a general can run a war without direct intervention of the political level,[13] as suggested by Jomini. The war also marked a continuity of policy, controlled by politics, as suggested by Clausewitz; this fact was proven possible by the teamwork of General Colin Powell as Chairman of the Joint Chiefs of Staff at the strategic-political level, which allowed General Norman H. Schwarzkopf to direct the war at the operational level. The much-touted public partnership of Powell and Schwarzkopf neglected any mention of the real strategy put in place behind the scenes by those at

---

[10] John A. Nagl, *Learning to Eat Soup with a Knife: Counterinsurgency Lessons from Malaya and Vietnam* (University of Chicago Press, 2005), 207. "AirLand Battle" was a Jominian concept that placed too much emphasis on the operational level of war, however effective, but which gave a template for the use of forces from the operational level toward the tactical level and took little heed of the political-strategic context.

[11] Kaplan, Fred M. *The Insurgents: David Petraeus and the Plot to Change the American Way of War* (New York: Simon & Schuster, 2013), 50–51.

[12] Clausewitz, *On War*, 75.

[13] Anthony H. Cordesman and Abraham R. Wagner, *The Lessons of Modern War, Vol. IV* (Boulder, CO; London: Westview Press, 1990), 233.

the senior-most levels of government. This fact also demonstrated that effective political control is not only possible but necessary to avoid a conflict that becomes "mindless and headless, [as] it is then that war assumes that absolute form that Clausewitz dreaded."[14]

Such control sadly was not achieved in more recent conflicts. After the success of the First Gulf War and the ongoing RMA, the concept of "AirLand Battle" underwent an escalation and malformation that resulted in the new "Shock and Awe" doctrine (also known as "Rapid Dominance") written about by Harlan K. Ullman and James P. Wade in the late 1990s.[15] According to these authors,

The basis for Rapid Dominance rests in the ability to affect the will, perception, and understanding of the adversary through imposing sufficient Shock and Awe to achieve the necessary political, strategic, and operational goals of the conflict or crisis that led to the use of force. War, of course, in the broadest sense has been characterized by Clausewitz to include substantial elements of "fog, friction, and fear." In the Clausewitzian view, "Shock and Awe" were necessary effects arising from application of military power and were aimed at destroying the will of an adversary to resist.[16]

Such concepts as "AirLand Battle" and "Shock and Awe" are iterations of a Jominian concept, covered with a Clausewitzian sugar coating, to be applied from the operational level down. They are doctrinal textbooks by which training may be developed and conducted, but they are not strategy. Emile Simpson pointed out, in *War from the Ground Up: Twenty-First Century Combat as Politics,* that strategy cannot be defined in advance, and strategy is geographically dependent: "For the mature Clausewitz, policy came first; principles should be adapted to form an operational plan tailored to a particular problem, understood on its own terms."[17] Hence, doctrines prepared for symmetrical fighting in Europe may not work somewhere else—especially if the

---

[14] Paret, Craig, and Gilbert, *Makers of Modern Strategy,* 865–66.

[15] Harlan Ullman and James P. Wade, *Shock and Awe: Achieving Rapid Dominance* (Washington, DC: National Defense University Center for Advanced Concepts and Technology, 1996).

[16] Ullman and Wade, *Shock and Awe,* 19.

[17] Simpson, *War from the Ground Up,* 135.

policies that frame the use of legitimate forces are not adapted to the peculiar environment in which the war has to be won. Andrew Bacevich put it more boldly in *Breach of Trust*: "With the passing of the Cold War, the last vestige of coherence [in strategy] vanished,"[18] a sentiment echoed by Strachan, as well: "The rhetoric of the war on terror stepped in to the black hole created by the bankruptcy of strategic thought at the end of the Cold War."[19]

2. On Counterinsurgency

Particularly in the post-9/11 environments of Iraq and Afghanistan, guerrilla and irregular war was more likely to arise after the end of military operations or even within military operations. The records of both the First World War and Second World War make this connection clear enough. An evolution toward insurgency was foreseeable, especially when there was no contingency plan to ameliorate citizens' everyday lives during the liberation of Iraq and Afghanistan. The liberator was now an occupying force. Once again, the local populace took arms to repulse or unseat the invader over time.

Jomini acknowledged that an insurgency may be a "'last and desperate resort' of an otherwise defeated people," but dismissed it; on the other hand, Clausewitz both recognized and appreciated it.[20] In *On War,* Clausewitz explains the basics of insurgency[21] and strategic and tactical problems for both sides. Long forgotten since the 1960s when first written, Werner Hahlweg gives an excellent summary in his classic article from the *Journal of Strategic Studies.*[22] Antulio J. Echevarria II, however, in "4th Generation-Warfare and Other Myths," explains how the trinity of chance, reason, and anger and hatred—

---

[18] Andrew J. Bacevich, *Breach of Trust: How Americans Failed Their Soldiers and Their Country* (New York: Metropolitan Books, 2013), 180.

[19] Hew Strachan, *The Direction of War: Contemporary Strategy in Historical Perspective* (New York: Cambridge University Press, 2013), 109.

[20] Freedman, Strategy, 179.

[21] Clausewitz, *On War*, especially Book VI, Chapters VIII, XXV, and XXVI.

[22] Werner Hahlweg, "Clausewitz and Guerrilla Warfare," *Journal of Strategic Studies* 9 no. 2–3 (1986), 127–33, doi:10.1080/01402398608437262.

rejected by van Creveld as outdated—is in fact still germane to insurgency.[23]

One can make an analytical framework of introspection based on Clausewitz's trinity to analyze deficiencies in counterinsurgencies. Within "Chances" can be regrouped the strategic blunders and their reasons; in "Reasons," policy and strategic-political gaps, and finally in "Hatred" the societal effects.

a.   The Role of Chance

After the events of September 11, 2001, Shock and Awe proved to be initially efficient in Iraq and Afghanistan, at least until the end of the military operations under Phase III. However, this concept did not properly address the problem of counterinsurgency and the realities of irregular warfare in either their classic or postmodern forms. The principles of Shock and Awe, with massive American firepower working against an adversary using symmetrical means in his way of fighting—that is, with traditional armies going at each other—fits a Jominian approach to fighting. Sir Hew Strachan described the dilemma in Afghanistan and Iraq: "The military instruments to which they entrusted their intentions were, however, designed for somewhat different undertaking from those to which the armed forces of America and Britain found themselves committed."[24]

In the face of insurgency and terrorism in such places as Afghanistan and Iraq,[25] the application of force is secondary to understanding the political, cultural, social, and economic dynamics of the environment that result in this resistance. The environment for insurgency is shaped by two major factors: politics and the targeted use of violence. Counterinsurgency is highly politicized;[26] therefore, military means

---

[23] Antulio Joseph Echevarria and U.S. Army War College, "Fourth-Generation War and Other Myths" (Carlisle Barracks, PA: Strategic Studies Institute, U.S. Army War College, 2005), 7.

[24] Strachan, *Direction of War,* 65.

[25] The misuse of firepower has proven to be detrimental in the past in other countries, such as India, Ireland, and Indochina.

[26] Kaplan, *Insurgents,* 164.

alone will not suffice to end the conflict.[27] Contrary to the school of counterinsurgency (COIN) that emerged in the United States at the time of the Iraqi surge around 2006, counterinsurgency is not a special case of war,[28] but a continuum in the spectrum of violence. Insurgency is the pivot point between police actions and de-escalation of the conflict and a renewed escalation toward a "symmetrical" war.

b. The Role of Reason

To resolve insurgencies, there must be a two-way bridge between the operational and political-strategic levels for strategy to also be efficient at the tactical level. Hew Strachan,[29] Colonel Gian Gentile,[30] and Emil Simpson[31] all argue in favor of this flow; their works embody some of the most informed and useful writings to emerge from the present era of conflict and strategic thought. They also illustrate the difference between the theoretical and practical approach to war of Jomini and Clausewitz. Because Jomini does not reflect on the effects of policies in war, applying his principles does not provide a direct answer to fix the two-way bridge.

However, an answer can be found in the more philosophical approach taken by Clausewitz. In Afghanistan and Iraq, there was not only a problem of choice between Jomini or Clausewitz, but the lack of a plan for "Phase IV," which resulted in the intrinsic demise of the Coalition.[32]

c. Hatred

A seemingly impossible task given to the armed forces, such as nation-building, can be detrimental to the two-way bridge. To under-

---

[27] Kaplan, *Insurgents*, 159.

[28] Ibid., 362.

[29] Strachan, *Direction of War*, 23–24.

[30] Gian Gentile, *Wrong Turn: America's Deadly Embrace of Counterinsurgency* (New York: The New Press, 2013), 118.

[31] Simpson, *War from the Ground Up*, 191–92.

[32] Michael R. Gordon and Bernard E. Trainor, *Cobra II: The Inside Story of the Invasion and Occupation of Iraq* (New York: Pantheon Books, 2006), 576.

stand the perspective of the armed forces, the analysis done in the 1980s by Peter Paret, Gordon A. Craig, and Felix Gilbert in *Makers of Modern Strategy* is noteworthy: "[Clausewitz's] criticism of attitudes and policies that he blamed for the defeat was harsh: the government had not used war as an instrument of foreign policy, but allowed itself to be isolated from prospective allies, and then gave its soldiers an impossible task."[33] Out of this impossible task was born the familiar myth of the "stab in the back," recounted in *Cobra II*, *The Insurgents*, *Learning to Eat Soup With a Knife*, and other works—but refuted almost solely by Frank Ledwidge in *Losing Small Wars*.[34] This troubling myth was already reinforced in Clausewitz's time by the inertia of society, resented by the military: "The country regarded the war as a matter for the army alone."[35] Societal inertia is the postulate of Andrew Bacevich in *Breach of Trust* when he reminds readers that only a meager one percent of the American population served its country in combat in the last decade-and-a-half, and few veterans today are influential in Washington politics.[36]

On the other side, to understand the insurgencies' views, Ledwidge, Simpson, Strachan, and Kaplan show how the misuse of firepower and the lack of restraint in the use of force led to a cycle of violence—a syndrome that recalls the U.S. experience of combat in Vietnam in the 1960s and 1970s.

In *On War*, Clausewitz had already identified this cycle: "We must consider [i.e., think carefully about] 'repaying atrocity with atrocity, violence with violence!'"[37] This violence leads to an unsecure environment in which trust and stability cannot develop the necessary conditions to move toward nation-building.[38]

---

[33] Paret, Craig, and Gilbert, *Makers of Modern Strategy*, 191–92.

[34] Frank Ledwidge, *Losing Small Wars: British Military Failure in Iraq and Afghanistan* (New Haven, CT: Yale University Press, 2012).

[35] Paret, Craig, and Gilbert, *Makers of Modern Strategy*, 192.

[36] Bacevich, *Breach of Trust*, 35, 43.

[37] Hahlweg, "Clausewitz and Guerrilla Warfare," 129.

[38] Gordon and Trainor, *Cobra II*, 574–75.

F. RESEARCH DESIGN

The methodology of this research is qualitative and entails three phases:

- to research the selected historical and empirical literature for the book, demonstrating Clausewitz's influences or absences thereof in the last decades' conflicts;
- to map the path by which Clausewitz's influences arose; and
- to compare, contrast, summarize and critically assess the adaptations and impacts in policy, strategy, and doctrine focused on counterinsurgency for English-speaking nations as well as Europe.

Since the 19th century, the subject of Clausewitz in U.S. strategic thought has been controversial, especially in the present generation. The majority of the literature concerning Clausewitz's influences is descriptive and based on secondary sources, military articles, and historical accounts. Various scholars, journalists, and military leaders have recounted direct or indirect influences with more or less detail. Therefore, the second chapter of this book discusses the available descriptive literature focusing on Clausewitz's influence in English-speaking nations, with a primary focus on the United States and the United Kingdom until 2001. It appears that Clausewitz is alive and well in the military but still in direct competition with a more Jominian approach of war that conflicts with the traditional chain of command. The second chapter concludes that the U.S. armed forces, although using Clausewitz, still fight a Jominian form of war. The conflictual relationship between the operational and strategic levels of war represented by these two military theorists results in a dichotomy which is at the heart of the problem when approaching COIN operations.

The third chapter briefly reviews Clausewitz's influence on strategic thought in Europe. It traces Clausewitz's influences in Europe in the post–World War II period through the development of the North Atlantic Treaty Organisation (NATO). During the last two decades, the United States and its European allies have demonstrated a divergence of views on multiple occasions on strategic issues, especially on how to approach the Afghanistan and Iraq conflicts. The third chapter concludes that, although the allies did not have the same strategic school of thought at the beginning of NATO, today they operate under a Clausewitzian, and not a Jominian, approach to war at a military-strategic level.

The fourth chapter compares and contrasts Clausewitz's *On War* with today's literature in order to highlight similarities and differences, with a special focus on COIN. This chapter concludes that Clausewitz's theories remain relevant within the whole spectrum of military operations, including COIN. Second, it proposes that COIN is not a separate art of war; rather COIN is a pivot in military operations along a continuum of violence. COIN operates at the juncture between escalation and de-escalation, and therefore it represents the "graduate-level warfare,"[39] as General Petraeus and John Nagl remarked, because military might is not enough to solve the problem alone; a DIME approach is necessary.

The fifth chapter explores selected effects, implications, and consequences for future military operations. It concludes that, in part, the answers to the conflicts in Afghanistan and Iraq were contained in *On War*, but were not recognized as such.

Finally, this book concludes that instead of scholars debating whether Jomini or Clausewitz should have been followed in Afghanistan and Iraq, it is time to go back to *Art of War* and *On War* to understand their complementary relationship in—and to—the 21st century. Classic strategic theory retains its value, despite the changing face of conflict.

---

[39] Cited in Kaplan, *Insurgents*, 164.

II. CLAUSEWITZ'S INFLUENCE IN THE UNITED STATES BEFORE 2001

Clausewitz percolated into the United States through a slow process, which has spanned over almost a century. As such, his influence is more subtle. In contrast, Baron Jomini's theories and thoughts comprise a majority of U.S. military thought and practice of strategy.[40] Quoting John Shy from two decades earlier, Colin S. Gray remarked in 2006 that, "Alas the spirit of Baron Antoine Henri de Jomini is alive and well and inhabits Washington, D.C. It was the spirit of his theory that gave us a technical and utterly apolitical understanding of strategic stability during the Cold War."[41] Gray's controversial but nonetheless accurate view of the matter derives from the foundation of West Point in the early 19th century, its board principally composed of such French immigrants as Claudius Crozet, Pierre Thomas, and Claudius Berard. At this time in much of Europe and in the young United States, French was the preeminent language of higher education. Thus, almost all military and strategy books at West Point were in or translated from French, and little if any attention was given to German literature.

According to Bruno Colson in *La Culture Stratégique Américaine*, the French, and presently the English-speaking world, only discovered Clausewitz after 1870, with the wars of German unification and the foundation of Germany's Second Reich.[42] However, Clausewitz's theories thereafter slowly spread from the old continent to the new, principally through British writers and German immigrants. Eventually, they reached the U.S. Military Academy (USMA), at least in part. Key in this connection was the path blazed by General Emory Upton as an influential admirer of the German military school. Christopher Bassford, in *Clausewitz in English: The Reception of Clausewitz in Britain and America 1815–1945*, does a remarkable job of tracing how Clausewitz was received in the New World—and through which

---

[40] Colson, *La Culture Stratégique Américaine*.

[41] Colin S. Gray, "Out of the Wilderness: Prime-Time for Strategic Culture," in *Support of the U.S. Nuclear Strategy Forum*, July 2006, https://fas.org/irp/agency/dod/dtra/stratcult-out.pdf, 4.

[42] Colson, *La Culture Stratégique Américaine*, 50.

channels. However, Bassford does not really tell his readers when, in an historical sense, Clausewitz began to influence U.S. military thought.

This chapter endeavors to build on Bassford's work with the specific point of identifying when and how Clausewitz's influence spread to the United States. Not surprisingly, Clausewitz first registered among scholars of war and strategy, and his works have had enduring effects on the several services of the U.S. armed forces as well as in the thinking and writing of notable military figures. While the reception of Clausewitz's strategic treatises in society at large has waxed and waned in response to the American experience of conflict and certain developments within academe, this chapter also traces the influence of Clausewitz in broader U.S. policy circles. Although Clausewitz's percolation into the United States was slow, it remains influential at the three levels of war.

A.   CLAUSEWITZ IN THE U.S. MILITARY

One of the first references to Clausewitz came from General Henry Wager Halleck, to whom some refer as the father of the U.S. strategy. Specifically, Halleck suggested the central role of "writing from Clausewitz" in his *Elements of Military Art and Science*, published in 1846.[43] The volume was used as a core text at the USMA—but it includes no excerpts, citations, or references from Clausewitz in the text.[44] Similarly, contemporary scholars have debated the Jominian or Clausewitzian way of war during the 1861–1865 U.S. Civil War and thereby define Generals Grant and Sherman as followers of a Clausewitzian way of war.

The historical record provides no evidence that these two generals ever read Clausewitz, however.[45] The reason is simple: There was no

---

[43] Henry Wagner Halleck, *Elements of Military Art and Science; or, Course of Instruction in Strategy, Fortification, Tactics of Battles, &c.; Embracing the Duties of Staff, Infantry, Cavalry, Artillery, and Engineers. Adapted to the Use of Volunteers and Militia* (New York: D. Appleton & Co., 1846), https://archive.org/details/elementsofmilita00hall, 59, 60, 154.

[44] Colson, *La Culture Stratégique Américaine*, 72.

[45] Ibid., 83, 154.

English translation of this work at this time. The first translation of *On War* was done by Colonel James John Graham in 1878,[46] thirteen years *after* the U.S. Civil War. It is thus unlikely that many American strategic thinkers had taken note of any of Clausewitz's texts except, perhaps, by reputation.

The advent of German unity in 1871 and the rise of a new generation of officers in the U.S. Army was exemplified by General Emory Upton. Upton went to Germany instead of France in 1876 and came back very much impressed with his experience at the Berliner Militärakademie in the young Second Reich.[47] Although there is no record of Upton reading Clausewitz,[48] one may assume that he was certainly exposed to Clausewitz during his time at the Berliner Militärakademie.

Only with *The Principles of Strategy,* written by Captain John Bigelow in 1894, does an explicit and complete reference to Clausewitz's *On War* appear.[49] This document seems to mark the turning point from the overweening French influence in U.S. military thought toward a more German-inflected school.[50] Thereafter, references to Clausewitz began to flourish around 1909, the date of the edition of *On War* translated by T. Miller Maguire and Colonel F.N. Maude.

In the 1920s, in the attempt to adapt the experience of the Great War to military education, Clausewitz made his entry to the Command and General Staff School and the War College; his works became required reading to enter the War College in 1928.[51] There also existed in the 1920s a fairly vigorous exchange of German and U.S. officers in various roles, not the least growing out of the U.S. occupation role in the Rhineland, as well as the fascination felt in German society with U.S. industrial production. There was a limited, but no

---

[46] According to http://www.clausewitz.com/bibl/WhichTrans.htm, consulted 4/27/2015.

[47] Colson, *La Culture Stratégique Américaine*, 183.

[48] Christopher Bassford, *Clausewitz in English: The Reception of Clausewitz in Britain and America, 1815–1945* (New York: Oxford University Press, 1994), 70.

[49] Colson, *La Culture Stratégique Américaine*, 180.

[50] Ibid., 182.

[51] Ibid., 204, 223.

less important, exchange of German officers with the U.S. Army, as well, and there was a school of German officers who looked on both the United States and the Soviet Union (USSR) as models of war and society. The exchange with the United States was not nearly as intense as the secret rearmament in the USSR, but the American fascination adhered on both sides—and encouraged more people to read Clausewitz.

1. **Clausewitz and the Generals**

Authors disagree on the importance, if any, of *On War* to Eisenhower during World War II. But According to Colson and confirmed by Christopher Bassford, Eisenhower did read the treatise at least three times in the 1920s, especially as his mentor George C. Marshall was famous as a figure who up-ended military education and training with new approaches.[52] Carlo d'Este reports that "when, toward the end of his life, Eisenhower was asked to name the most influential military book he had ever read, he unhesitatingly replied that it was Carl von Clausewitz's classic study, *On War*."[53]

When Eisenhower was appointed Chief of War Plans by Marshall in 1942, Colonel Albert C. Wedmeyer was his second. The interaction between Eisenhower and Wedmeyer, who studied at the German Kriegsakademie in Berlin in 1936–1938 (where Clausewitz was a part of the curriculum), is also an interesting link to the Clausewitz's influence in the 1940s, directly at the heart of the U.S. military system. On the other hand, Jim deFelice in *Omar Bradley: General at War*, suggests that neither General Bradley nor General Patton seemed to have been fervent admirers of Clausewitz;[54] nevertheless, Patton did read *On*

---

[52] Colson, *La Culture Stratégique Américaine*, 208.

[53] Carlo D'Este, *Eisenhower: A Soldier's Life* (New York: Henry Holt & Co., 2002), 168.

[54] Jim deFelice, *Omar Bradley: General at War* (Washington, DC: Regnery History, 2011), https://books.google.com/books?id=Ycgu_Kmq5YgC&pg=PT250&dq=Jim+deFelice+in+Omar+Bradley:+General+at+War+Clausewitz&hl=en&sa=X&ved=0CCUQ6AEwAGoVChMIspLDzefyyAIVxTaICh2liA1A#v=onepage&q=Jim%20deFelice%20in%20Omar%20Bradley%3A%20General%20at%20War%20Clausewitz&f=false.

War at the same period that Eisenhower did. Eisenhower, through his career as a general and as a president later, may mark the turning point to a more Clausewitzian approach in the country's politics.

Samuel Huntington reflected a mid-20th century view and its optimism when we wrote, "Military chiefs held too much power, which expanded beyond the military domain into diplomacy, politics and economics."[55] This fact is why Generals Eisenhower and MacArthur were successful in their time. In World War II, they could locally coordinate diplomacy with strategy, strategy with regional politics, then regional politics with the operational level within the strategic atmosphere of the United States. However, President Roosevelt kept them in check with the help of General Marshall, who personally knew both Eisenhower and, particularly, MacArthur; they had worked closely in France during World War I.[56] It is also noteworthy that both military leaders served together in the Philippines before 1940, Eisenhower under MacArthur, in the expeditionary forces. Their relationships were not perfect, but they did learn how to understand and to run a defeated and subject country, experience that eventually contributed to their respective successes in Europe and Japan in 1942–1950.

Clausewitz has left a mark on individual military leaders more heavily since the 1980s than before because the text existed in an easily usable form. For example, General Colin Powell recalls *On War* being "like a beam of light from the past, illuminating present-day military quandaries."[57] Melton hails General Schwarzkopf as "an adherent to the Clausewizian paradigm that pervaded the army's doctrine in the 1980s."[58] He has a similar assessment of General Tommy

---

[55] Simpson, *War from the Ground Up*, 113.

[56] Paul H. Jeffers, *Marshall: Lessons in Leadership* (New York: Palgrave Macmillan, 2010), 50.

[57] Cited in Daniel Treisman, "Clausewitz in Afghanistan," University of California, Los Angeles, http://www.sscnet.ucla.edu/polisci/faculty/treisman/Papers/clause.pdf.

[58] Stephen L. Melton, *The Clausewitz Delusion: How the American Army Screwed Up the War in Iraq and Afghanistan* (Minneapolis: Zenith Press, 2009), 112.

Franks: "Franks, like so many other officers of his military generation, was a Clausewitzian."[59]

2. Clausewitz and the Services

Although the Army was, through Summers' book, the main motor of transformation, it is the Marine Corps that adapted the most to Clausewitz among the several services. The Air Force and the Navy were also affected at different level, but not as much as the USMC and the U.S. Army.

Clausewitz's real influence on the U.S. Army can be traced to the early 1980s; Colonel Huba Wass de Czege, largely influenced by Clausewitz, was instrumental in the conception of the "AirLand Battle" doctrine, on which "Rapid Dominance," perhaps better known as the Shock and Awe doctrine, is another iteration. This concept is even more clearly based on Clausewitz. Still, although the concepts are Clausewitzian in essence, their interpretations remain more Jominian.

At the same time in mid-'80s, the U.S. Marine Corps, according to Major Ben Connable in "Culture Warriors: Marine Corps Organizational Culture and Adaptation to Cultural Terrain, was also incorporating Clausewitz in its way of war:

The vehicle for transformation came in 1985 with the publication of Bill Lind's *Maneuver Warfare Handbook*. Maneuver Warfare was not a revolutionary concept. Lind essentially boiled down the time-tested warfighting philosophies of Sun Tzu, Carl von Clausewitz, and Colonel John Boyd and situated them in the context of the decentralized tactical theory of the World War I and II German Armies.[60]

Furthermore, Bassford confirms that the noteworthy 1989 doctrinal manual FMFM-1 is a "Condensation of Clausewitz"[61] and therefore marks the point of entry of Clausewitzian influence in the modern doctrine of the U.S. Marine Corps. Stuart Kinross argues that

---

[59] Melton, *The Clausewitz Delusion*, 116.

[60] Ben Connable, "Culture Warriors: Marine Corps Organizational Culture and Adaptation to Cultural Terrain," *Small War Journal* (February 7, 2008), http://smallwarsjournal.com/jrnl/art/culture-warriors, 8.

[61] Bassford, *Clausewitz in English*, 205.

under the influence of General Charles Krulak, Captain John Schmitt continued to develop a more Clausewitzian view of the FMFM-1 with the Marine Corps Doctrinal Publication (MCDP) 1 *Warfighting* and then the MCDP 1–1 *Strategy* authored by Christopher Bassford in 1997.[62]

Clausewitz's influence in the U.S. Navy is a little hazier because of the role of naval strategic theory and its connections to classical theory with an emphasis on continental Europe. Although Navy doctrine is based on Mahan, himself an unabashed advocate of Jomini, it certainly was also influenced in 1905 by Clausewitz in an indirect way. According to Christopher Bassford,[63] Clausewitz's writing may have made its way to the United States through articles from Rear-Admiral Baron Curt von Maltzahn, translated and published in English at the Royal Navy's War College[64] and by an earlier English translation of the Russian Admiral S. O. Makarov's work on naval tactics in 1898.[65] Such British admirals as Philip Howard, James Thursfield and Julian Corbett, who were read in the United States, were also influenced indirectly by Clausewitz in their work. Although Alfred Thayer Mahan based his work on Jomini, he recognized Clausewitz as "one of the first authorities,"[66] though he appears only to have read it later, around 1910.[67] Dr Steven Metz confirms that "the Maritime Strategy was Clausewitzian even though Mahan was the Navy's patron saint."[68]

---

[62] Stuart Kinross, *Clausewitz and America: Strategic Thought and Practice from Vietnam to Iraq* (London: Routledge, 2008), 190.

[63] Bassford, *Clausewitz in English*, 94–95.

[64] Ibid., 244. Admiral von Maltzahn, trans. W.H. Hancock, *What Lesson has General von Clausewitz's Work, "On War," for the Naval Officer?* (Portsmouth: War College, November 1906), No.4 (Naval Library P806); originally *Marine Rundschau*, June 1905.

[65] Ibid. Vice Admiral S.O. Makarov, Imperial Russian Navy, *Discussion of Questions in Naval Tactics*, trans. Lieutenant [USN] John B. Bernadou (Washington, DC: Office of Naval Intelligence, 1898; reprinted Annapolis: United States Naval Institute, 1990).

[66] Cited in Bassford, *Clausewitz in English*, 95.

[67] Colson, *La Culture Stratégique Américaine*, 197.

[68] Dr. Steven Metz cited in Kinross, *Clausewitz and America*, 117.

For the U.S. Air Force, Clausewitz appears in writings from Major General Haywood S. Hansell and also in the works of General John Ashley Warden III. According to Stuart Kinross, the 1984 Air Force Manual 1–1 reflects a Clausewitzian approach[69] and moreover, Lieutenant-Colonel Barry Watts and the fine work of Major Mark Clodfelter that debunked the air war in Vietnam based their reflections on the Air Force for their works on Clausewitz.[70] For Bassford, the impact on the doctrine is "less clear,"[71] but is still basically Clausewitzian for Kinross.

B. CLAUSEWITZ AND U.S. READERS

Clausewitz did not only capture the attention of the U.S. armed forces and their personnel; scholars also played an important role in disseminating Clausewitz more broadly. Few did more in this regard than the Stanford and Princeton scholar Peter Paret. Bassford seems to think that the group who participated in the "Clausewitz Project" at Princeton—originally an attempt to translate the body of Clausewitz's work—laid the foundation for a larger interest in *On War*.[72] Two other influential works also helped in this direction even earlier—Samuel Huntington's *The Soldier and the State*"[73] in 1957, and Robert E. Osgood's *Limited War*,[74] which Bassford considered "breakthroughs" in spreading a positive image of Clausewitz in the United States at a scholarly level.

To illustrate how Clausewitz came to influence U.S. military thinking, one may turn to more tangible and visual data in our era of big

---

[69] Kinross, *Clausewitz and America*, 112.

[70] Bassford, *Clausewitz in English*, 204; Kinross, *Clausewitz and America*, 112.

[71] Bassford, *Clausewitz in English*, 204.

[72] Ibid., 207. Carl von Clausewitz, *On War*, ed. and trans. Michael Howard and Peter Paret (Princeton, NJ: Princeton University Press, 1976).

[73] Samuel P. Huntington, *The Soldier and the State: The Theory and Politics of Civil-military Relations* (Cambridge, Mass.: Belknap Press of Harvard University Press, 1957).

[74] Robert Endicott Osgood, *Limited War: The Challenge to American Strategy* ([Chicago]: University of Chicago Press, 1957).

data. A research on Google Ngram Viewer for Jomini and Clausewitz led to the graphic in Figure 1.

Figure 1, Clausewitz vs. Jomini in the English-Speaking World

Source: Ngram Viewer,[75] Analysis of the relative frequency of words in printed documents from 1800 to 2008 in books and in English for Jomini and Clausewitz.

This chart is interesting first because it shows Jomini "losing" general interest over the years in favor of Clausewitz, who is gaining.

Second, the peaks in Clausewitz's popularity show some very interesting correlations. By 1909, the influence of the first English translation of *On War* by T. Miller McGuire is manifest in the first time that Clausewitz passes over the Jomini line in terms of mention and readership. The progression continues with a first peak by 1917 or so, corresponding to the end of the First World War. Then, a diminishing interest amid interwar peace until the late 1930s was followed by a second peak during WWII; the 1943 edition of *On War* actually marks the decline of interest for Clausewitz in this period,

---

[75] Ngram Viewer graphic, accessed May 4, 2015,
https://books.google.com/ngrams/graph?content=Jomini%2Cjomini%2CClausewitz%2Cclausewitz&year_start=1800&year_end=2015&corpus=15&smoothing=3&share=&direct_url=t1%3B%2CJomini%3B%2Cc0%3B.t1%3B%2Cjomini%3B%2Cc0%3B.t1%3B%2CClausewitz%3B%2Cc0%3B.t1%3B%2Cclausewitz%3B%2Cc0

coupled with the fatigue of the war, followed by a diminishing interest again until the 1950s. A new cycle, starting with the Korean War, marks the next increase in interest, with the next apogee in the 1970s.

Clausewitz's prominence fell off again with the end of the Vietnam War, but renewed interest seems to correspond somewhat with Peter Paret's 1976 edition of *On War*. Paret's work rendered Clausewitz accessible and affordable to the American public, who were in search of answers in the wake of defeat in Vietnam. The mood in the aftermath of the Vietnam War was instrumental in the spreading of *On War* through the military, scholarly, and political realms. The military leadership, eager to understand the causes of failure in Vietnam, used Clausewitz to delve into the nature of war and the causes of military failure in the wake of such victories earlier in the century.

The most famous of these figures, Colonel Harry Summers, based his analysis of the Vietnam War on Clausewitz in a study produced at the U.S. Army War College that became a best seller.[76] Summers' work and the subsequent efforts of other scholars in the 1970s and 1980s prompted a chain reaction at different levels.[77] An example is the work of Stephen L. Melton, *The Clausewitz Delusion: How the American Army Screwed up the War in Iraq and Afghanistan,* in which he recognizes the transition to Clausewitz in the late 1970s: "*On War* became the army's new intellectual touchstone,"[78] though he continues that "reinventing ourselves as nineteenth-century Prussians [sic] was perhaps the worst way to resolve the army's post-Vietnam crisis."[79] Melton argues against what he perceives as a resurgence of Romanticism for a more scientific way of war.

Melton argues for a more "engineering approach,"[80] in other words, for a status quo of technology and firepower as well as metrics in guerilla war that ignore the political. Robert McNamara took such an approach and it did not work as expected in a time of managerial

---

[76] Harry G. Summers, *On Strategy: The Vietnam War in Context* (Carlisle Barracks, PA: Washington, D.C.: Strategic Studies Institute, U.S. Army War College, 1981).

[77] Bassford, *Clausewitz in English*, 198–99, 204.

[78] Melton, *Clausewitz Delusion*, 4.

[79] Ibid., 4.

[80] Melton, *Clausewitz Delusion*, 4.

optimism and American strategic ascendancy. This intensely odd argument is totally ahistorical, as the system engineering approach that McNamara had manifested in his stewardship of the Department of Defense (DOD) and Vietnam had itself been regarded at the time, by the Viet Cong as well as McNamara's critics, as a manifest failure.

Clausewitz suffered an abrupt loss in readership in the early 1980s until the publication of Colonel Summers's work in 1981, reinforced by the second edition of *On War* by Paret in 1984, culminating again in the beginning of the 1990s, with the First Gulf War and general interest in war and politics in the waning of the Cold War era.

By 1991—with the end of the Cold War, the rise of warfare in the Middle East as the central front of world conflict, the advent of the militarily inexperienced Clinton administration, and the influential book written by Martin van Creveld, *The Transformation of War*—Clausewitz lost his momentum for a decade, marking the beginning of the last visible cycle before the turn of the century. There followed a new peak after the events of the 9/11. Hew Strachan makes a further connection between causes and effects: "Because Summers was important to Petraeus's thesis, so was Clausewitz."[81] In other words, Summers was instrumental to the propagation of Clausewitz's influence in the last generation of generals because of his significant role in 1976 fashioning the first doctrinal answer to the collapse in Indochina.

In comparison, in the German-speaking world, Clausewitz was both more widely and more consistently read, as shown in Figure 2.

---

[81] Strachan, *Direction of War*, 62.

Figure 2, Clausewitz vs. Jomini in German-Speaking World

Source: Ngram Viewer,[82] Analysis of the relative frequency of words in printed documents from 1800 to 2008 in books and in German for Clausewitz and Jomini.

In German literature, Clausewitz has tended to appear more frequently before a war, for example, in 1869, about one year before the 1870 Franco-Prussian War. In 1911, the writing on Clausewitz start to peak again, three years before World War I, and the last relevant peak started in 1929, almost a decade before World War II started in Europe. Then two peaks appear with the start and the end of the Cold War; since then, he has been in decline. This trajectory shows a totally different picture from the U.S. patterns.

C. CLAUSEWITZ IN U.S. POLICY AND STRATEGY

In the nuclear age under Eisenhower's presidency from 1953 until 1961, Clausewitz's ideas started to permeate through political decision-making especially concerning nuclear policy. Regarding nuclear strategy in the classical period of the 1950s and the 1960s, Henry

---

[82] Ngram Viewer graphic, accessed May 4, 2015, https://books.google.com/ngrams/graph?content=Clausewitz%2C+jomini&case_insensitive=on&year_start=1800&year_end=2008&corpus=20&smoothing=3&share=&direct_url=t1%3B%2CClausewitz%3B%2Cc0%3B.t1%3B%2CJomini%3B%2Cc0.

Kissinger is hailed as neo-Clausewitzian, as was Hermann Kahn. Scholars debate whether Kissinger and Kahn were Clausewitzian themselves, but if a link can be established, it is in their apparent understanding that a nuclear war was a continuity of a state policy by other means.[83] In this same period of time, the nuclear strategist Bernard Brodie became a central person as the historian and nuclear strategist at the RAND Corporation with broad influence on the U.S. services, especially on the U.S. Air Force and the U.S. Navy.

Inside the policy realm, perhaps the most striking result of Clausewitz's rise is first seen in the post-Vietnam period with the Weinberger Doctrine of 1984, which ultimately became the Powell-Weinberger Doctrine. Both doctrines are influenced by Vietnam's aftermath of irregular conflict as well as the institutional imperative to reconstruct the forces, and, of course, the work of Summers.[84] They link military action with policy and the trinity. However, voices like Colonel Philip Lisagor, among the most recent, in his article "Don't Bring Back the Powell Doctrine,"[85] argue that Powell-Weinberger[86] was not Clausewitzian per se, because it restricted the use of forces in comparison with other doctrines. These doctrines also do not accord to the spirit or even the letter of Clausewitz, as they skew the center of gravity of reason far, at the expense of the sovereign, and also seek to regulate anger and hatred in such a way that ends up being alien to the work of professional soldiers.

Nevertheless, Andreas Herberg Rothe, a student of Clausewitz specialist Werner Hahlweg, in is article "A Prussian in the United States," dismisses such critics in light of the successor to the office of the Secretary of Defense:

---

[83] Bassford, *Clausewitz in English*, 198–99, 201.

[84] Eric R. Alterman, "Thinking Twice: The Weinberger Doctrine and the Lessons of Vietnam," *The Fletcher Forum* (Winter 1986), 95.

[85] Philip Lisagor, "Don't Bring Back the Powell Doctrine," *Cicero Magazine* (February 11, 2015), http://ciceromagazine.com/opinion/dont-bring-back-the-powell-doctrine/.

[86] Powell Doctrine is characterized by clear political objectives determined in advance, overwhelming military force to achieve objectives, and a known exit strategy. Strachan, *Direction of War*, 19.

While the Weinberger-Powell doctrine understands war explicitly as the last resort of policy, that of [Donald] Rumsfeld could be summarized as: Do everything you need to do first. But this approach neglects any strategic dimension and especially the planning of the political and social circumstances of the situation after the war, the real purpose we are fighting for.[87]

If the Powell doctrine was deemed difficult in rendering the strategic dialogue, Rumsfeld's doctrine alienates it. In the same period, at the political level, the Goldwater-Nichols act of 1986 prompted reforms of the armed forces in a Clausewitzian way, arguing for more "jointness" in the armed forces as well as what hoped to be a consolidation of the high command, the assignment of greater say to the regional or combatant commanders, and a stronger role for the chairman of the Joint Chiefs of Staff (JCS). The direct link from the president to the combatant commanders echoed the ideas of Clausewitz on political-military control and addressed the problematic role of the commander-in-chief, who is not the commander in the field, by the use of the Joint Chief of Staff as a special adviser. In Clausewitz's words, "Unless statesman and soldier are combined in one person, the only sound expedient is to make the commander-in-chief a member of the cabinet;"[88] Goldwater-Nichols addressed this issue as well as the enduring problem of overall strategy and theater operations in American military practice by reinforcing the role of the chairman of the JCS and the combatant commander.

Clausewitz also expressed that the military advisor should not only give military advice at this level, but also explains political repercussions.[89] In this respect, the Goldwater-Nichols Act is a demonstration of Clausewitz's influence at the policy level of the state. First, the president has a direct link with the theater level, close to the operations in the fields without "serious loss of time,"[90] as recommended

---

[87] Andreas Herberg Rothe, "A Prussian in the United States," *Europäische Sicherheit* (October 2003), http://www.clausewitz.com/readings/Herberg-Rothe/CWZintheUSA.htm.

[88] Clausewitz, *On War*, 608.

[89] Ibid., 607.

[90] Clausewitz, *On War*, 609.

by Clausewitz, to influence military actions. Second the JCS, having a larger view of the situation than, say, an army or air force regional headquarters, may advise on the implications of military action on the president's policy. However, Steve Willis in "Clausewitz and Corbett are Now Too Much" argues in a retrograde manner that the "defense reform efforts like the Goldwater-Nichols Act of 1986 reduced the power of service chiefs who traditionally formulated strategy."[91] This process is visible in the experience of the U.S. Navy in the last generation.

Today, the service chiefs are force providers and are responsible for doctrinal matters with an emphasis on the operational level and not strategy. The shaping of the strategy is in hands of the Joint Chiefs of Staff as member of the "cabinet" that advises the president and the Secretary of Defense and ultimately of the combatant commanders who implement the president's orders. In this respect, the link between policy at strategic level and military goals at the theater level is reinforced. What did not work recently was not a flaw in this reorganization at the JCS level, but the micromanagement from the military-political level in operational matters, as numerous authors point out, maybe the most influential being Fred Kaplan[92] and Michael Gordon.[93]

D. CLAUSEWITZ'S CRITICS

Clausewitz sparks a visceral reaction among many critics because Clausewitz's *On War* is analytical and not prescriptive. It does not contain a list nor does it contain the reductionist aphorisms of Sun Tzu or the diagrams and pleasing generalities of Jomini. The text imposes the need to think about war in its context, not to apply a recipe to win and because all wars are different in detail and appearance if not in their political nature, there is no single solution; like brewing beer, if one use the same malt, but a different water, the taste of the

---

[91] Steve Willis, "Clausewitz and Corbett are Now Too Much" (Center for International Maritime Security, March 5, 2015), http://cimsec.org/clausewitz-corbett-now-much/15338.

[92] Kaplan, *Insurgents*.

[93] Gordon and Trainor, *Cobra II*.

beer will change. People see Clausewitz *or* Jomini, but, in reality, there are few differences between Jomini and Clausewitz' theories. The strategists are complementary. For example, until the end of the Vietnam War, one can argue that the American Way of War was primarily Jominian. According to Eberstadt's report in 1945 and even Marshall later in 1956, American officers did not pay enough attention to the political objectives during WWII and their utility in military planning, with an over-emphasis on victory and firepower.[94]

Corn also recognizes it when he wrote, with a nod to the ill effect of Field Marshall Helmut von Moltke and MacArthur, "the Clausewitzian Dictum remains a valuable warning, especially in an American context where policy-makers and public opinion alike are too readily inclined to think of war as the *suspension* of politics."[95] This fact is explained by the Jominian's school of thought, which finally led to the Vietnam War and its result. As Colson writes, "There was a lack of strategic integration: purely military solutions were not linked to political solutions."[96]

This syndrome is best depicted by Summers' exchange with a North-Vietnamese colonel reported at the opening of the work *On Strategy*: "'You know you never defeated us on the battlefield,' said the American colonel. The North-Vietnamese colonel pondered this remark a moment. 'That may be so,' he replied, 'but it is also irrelevant.'"[97] North-Vietnam won on the political level and this is what it is now remembered. War starts and ends on political settlement and is a wedge to influence in one way or another the politics of the adversary. This dichotomy led soldiers and others to see war as separated from the political as well as the social and the cultural spheres, with the known results in Vietnam, but also in Iraq.

---

[94] Colson, *La Culture Stratégique Américaine*, 236.

[95] Tony Corn, "From Mars to Minerva: Clausewitz, Liddell Hart, and the Two Western Ways of War," *Small Wars Journal* (May 21, 2011), http://smallwarsjournal.com/, 6.

[96] Colson, *La Culture Stratégique Américaine*, 250.

[97] Cited by Lt. Gen. James M. Dubik, "Winning Battles, Losing Wars," *Army Magazine* (November 18, 2014), http://www.armymagazine.org/2014/11/18/winning-battles-losing-wars/#sthash.SPtDmfiy.dpbs%20.

When war is disconnected from its political ends, the idea that technology and firepower alone can win the war, like during the Vietnam War, flourished again during the last decade. With too little attention paid to the imponderable and by betting on the technological advances of the armed forces, decision-makers forget the importance of moral forces; thus, connecting war policy with the military realm did not attract as much interest.[98] The entire cosmos of religious-inspired terrorism or guerilla combat has over-taxed much of the military thought, with catastrophic effects.

E. CONCLUSION

Flag officers who were in command during the recent conflicts of the so-called Global War on Terror, like Generals Petraeus, Zinni, and McMaster, have also influenced the next potential generations of flag officers by their own works and publications. The adjunction of the National Security Affaires curriculum at the Naval Postgraduate School and the mandatory reading of Clausewitz's *On War* at the Naval War College are only two examples of many that Clausewitz is recognized by scholars and officers as relevant even today. Nevertheless, one struggles to pinpoint any change because of the number of documents and the cross-pollination of ideas since the mid-1980s until the publication of the FM 3–24 in late 2006.

The relative balance of ends and means present in the Gulf War (1990–1991) has vanished in the last decade, leading to a misreading of the kind of war in which the West has entered.[99] This author would argue with Kaplan and Gordon that the problem was less the democratic institutional-political overview of the military based on Clausewitz ideas, as many argue, than a problem of egos of personalities in command at the time. Added to this fact is the natural, modern tendency of those at the operational level of war to follow Moltke or even Schlieffen in the attempt to elevate a subordinate level of war to the highest level, especially in the face of the ambiguities of violence and politics.

---

[98] Bassford, *Clausewitz in English*, 205.
[99] Clausewitz, *On War*, 579.

To his credit, Corn calls for more "inter-agency jointness"[100] to create a holistic approach to war. However, his proposal to shift away from Clausewitz, demonstrates a misreading of the methodology given in *On War*. Clausewitz was also adamant that his work was not doctrinal; rather, he said that it should educate one's thoughts for the battlefield prior to an engagement—not thereafter.[101]

However, the differences between the German-speaking world and the English-speaking world graphics in this chapter suggests that Clausewitz's influence in the United States rose with a reversal of fate on the battlefield, which prompts questioning on how the United States "lost" a war but not the battles. The question embodies an apolitical and an engineering approach of the U.S. military culture that can be traced all the way back to West Point's inception and the Jominian influence from the beginning of the institution which permanently marked the way of war chosen by the United States in the past century, as argued by John Shy in the 1980s. But the engineering method of war in reality and war in theory cannot simplify the complexity of conflicts and requires a complementary approach to grasp the chances, hatred, and reasons of those conflicts.

Even if U.S. scholars and personalities promoted Clausewitz's *On War* in their own works, one may well argue that it is the force of war itself which led to Clausewitz's influences being promoted in American thought, and not the reverse. As a sound source of theory formulated to the needs of thought and practice, Clausewitz still influences U.S. military thought by an indirect approach, based on hard-learned lessons on the battlefields, instead of a top-down doctrinal process prior to a war.

---

[100] Corn, "From Mars to Minerva," 21.
[101] Clausewitz, *On War*, 141.

III. CLAUSEWITZ'S INFLUENCE IN EUROPE: THE ORACLE OF NATO

In conflicts since 1991, the United States and European countries have been working together in a "coalition of the willing" or under NATO. In this respect, if Clausewitz is relevant for the United States, he also should be relevant for Europe within NATO. Therefore, a short study of this organization is necessary to understand today's European view on strategy.

The North Atlantic Treaty demonstrates Clausewitz's core insight into the political nature of war as well as the dialectic of war in theory versus war in fact. Prior strategic schools of thought could not be pertinent to the needs of the Washington Treaty in the circumstances of the 1949 and thereafter as democracies pushed for a politically responsive and subordinate alliance system; hence, Clausewitz's school of thought was, in this case, a natural medium in which NATO could grow. This military-political dialogue is visible today in NATO structures and in its way of waging wars and approaching crises. To sustain this claim, this chapter explores NATO's past and its preparedness for defense (1949–1989) through its structural aspects. Then this chapter explores NATO's use of force to compel adversaries during the last two and a half decades (1990–2015) through some operational aspects and concludes that Clausewitz's *On War* is visible within NATO.

A. THE LONG ROAD TO NATO

In 1949, the North Atlantic Treaty Organization was founded as a means to extract and apply practical security and defense lessons from the recent war and to marshal the few available resources for the surviving democracies. NATO was born in a spirit of preparedness for defense by war-weary countries to counteract an ever-growing Soviet threat. In 1948–1949, none of the future members could have stood alone before the Soviet "red bear," which was anything but demobilized and thought to have nearly 5.5 million men,[102] or roughly 200 divisions, ready to sweep into central Europe. In the wake of the political and economic measures constituted in the Marshall Plan as well as the Brussels Pact, more steps were needed in the trans-Atlantic realm to assure the security of Western Europe and its recovery.

Continental Europeans, Canadians, Britons, and Americans came to the logical conclusion that an alliance was needed instead of a return to the failed diplomacy of the years 1919–1939. The choice of an alliance as a system of security and the defensive posture of this alliance can be seen, in a sense, as taking more than a page from Clausewitz. At that time, the security problem in Europe was reflected by Clausewitz's trinity of politics, the political-psychological forces readying for war, and in mass politics.

At the time, the American strategic school of thought was Jominian, in a conventional manner as the perpetuation of doctrine in military organizations is understood; this granted the French a legacy in the eighteenth and nineteenth centuries in American military experience. This was also true for the French. The British, another major ally, were following Basil Liddell Hart's doctrine, which was anti-Clausewitzian at heart, as well as anti-continental, and oriented toward an indirect approach to conflict, in opposition to both Jomini and Clausewitz. The Canadians, being held between the geographical American's hammer and the British relationship's anvil, were and still are, not exactly Clausewitzian.[103] Finally, at the time of NATO's creation, the West Germans were absent, only joining the Alliance in 1955, as new allies. In the 1950s, the Wehrmacht veterans in the new

---

[102] Mark A. Stoler, *Allies and Adversaries: The Joint Chiefs of Staff, the Grand Alliance, and U.S. Strategy in World War II* (Chapel Hill: University of North Carolina Press, 2000), 262.

[103] Major-General Éric Tremblay and Dr. Bill Bentley, "Canada's Strategic Culture: Grand Strategy and the Utility of Force," *Canadian Military Journal* 15, no. 3 (2015), http://www.journal.forces.gc.ca/vol15/no3/page5-eng.asp, 17. The reader is asked to take note of footnote 33, "Colin S. Gray, *The Strategy Bridge*..., p. 138. The work of Carl von Clausewitz is almost completely absent from Canadian military schools despite the fact that both Gray and Bernard Brodie have argued that Clausewitz is the closest that strategy's theorists have come to the status of Newton and Einstein. *On War* offers dicta that approximate the theories of gravity and relativity."

Bundeswehr knew of Clausewitz, but the Bundeswehr still thought in operational terms in addressing the Alliance's new strategic problems.

B.   PREPARATION FOR DEFENSE (1949–1989)

According to Håkan Edström and Dennis Gyllensporre in *Pursuing Strategy*, NATO went through three distinct periods.[104] The first period (1949–1969), as seen in four strategic concepts, pointed to the need for defense. The second period (1970–1990) did not see a single new strategic concept, which demonstrated a certain stability within the Alliance, while during the third period (1991–2011), three different strategic concepts were published, the last one being released in 2010. This last period pointed out NATO's need to adapt in order to survive. In this chapter, the author concentrates on this first period, while the next chapter deals more with the third period. The second period is not explored because of the absence of strategic concept.

In their quest for a new solution to their security dilemma, the mindset of NATO's founders reflects Clausewitz's conclusion of Chapter 3, "The Genius of War": "Experience and observation will both tell us that is the inquiring rather than creative minds, comprehensive rather than specialized, the calm rather than excitable heads to which in war we would choose to entrust the fate of our brothers and children, and the safety and the honor of our country."[105] As Clausewitz proposed, the Washington Treaty, also referred to as the North Atlantic Treaty, gave an "inquiring" posture to the Alliance, especially on other ways to promote democracy and peace instead of war. It imparted a "comprehensive" approach; the use of arms control and cooperation lent a more holistic approach to a lasting peace. The establishment of an Alliance before any conflict led to "calmness," enhanced by continual planning for and exercise of the worst-case scenarios. The structure of the North Atlantic Treaty also dem-

---

[104] Håkan Edström and Dennis Gyllensporre, *Pursuing Strategy* (February 2012), http://www.palgraveconnect.com/pc/doifinder/10.1057/9780230364196.0001, 6.

[105] Clausewitz, *On War*, 112.

onstrated genius and flexibility inside the Alliance to accommodate the political objectives of its Allies as for the French example.[106]

The first period of NATO starts with the Washington Treaty[107] and the foundation of NATO itself. Looking at the treaty itself, certain articles are more relevant than others for the following analysis in terms of unveiling the spirit of Clausewitz; therefore, not all will be cited. In the introduction, the notions of alliance, defense and territoriality are explicit, as well as what is considered to be both a set of common values and a trip-wire if attacked.[108]

Article One recognizes the body of international laws as fundamental for the North Atlantic Treaty and its operational legal frame, which echoed Clausewitz's "imperceptible limitations … known as international law and custom."[109]

Articles Two and Three stress the cooperative aspect of the Alliance, which appeal to Clausewitz's view of alliance, allies and the trinity, whereby the methods of political life in democracies are included in the body of the North Atlantic Treaty extracted from the Marshall Plan, and attention to the balance of ends and means.

Article Four gives the possibility for equal consultation, again with a political and pluralistic foundation.

Article Five is the collective defense core of the North Atlantic Treaty in event of an attack. Not only the Alliance's credibility rests upon this article, but the means and the end goals are explicit: "including the use of armed force, to restore and maintain the security of the North Atlantic area."[110] The passage also mentions the balance of means and ends and makes no automatic, unbinding commitment, based on the negative experience of the Covenant of the League and

---

[106] Ian Q. R. Thomas, *The Promise of Alliance: NATO and the Political Imagination* (Lanham, MA: Rowman and Littlefield, 1997), 90–91. The French withdrawal from the integrated military command structure is one example.

[107] North Atlantic Treaty Organisation (NATO), *The North Atlantic Treaty* (Washington, DC: April 4, 1949), http://www.nato.int/cps/en/natolive/official_texts_17120.htm.

[108] Thomas, *Promise of Alliance*, 72.

[109] Clausewitz, *On War*, 75.

[110] NATO, *North Atlantic Treaty*, art 5.

the U.S. Senate in 1920. Not only does it foresee the involvement of the Alliance's trinities in the decision to go to war, but it also attempts to focus on the capabilities to muster a "maximum exertion of strength."[111]

Article Five reflects what Clausewitz understood when he wrote, "The natural aim of military operation is the enemy's overthrow."[112] The next vital article is the ninth, which calls for the establishment of a representative council to "consider matters concerning the implementation of this Treaty,"[113] where all parties have to be represented. This article links the military-strategic sphere to the grand-strategy political sphere. In other words, the North Atlantic Treaty is a cooperative, defensive alliance under political control, which operates under international laws to maintain a set of values commonly recognized by the signatory nations. None of what preceded is Jominian, that is, there is neither emphasis on a single form of strategy as dominant in war, nor is the tactical level over-emphasized, nor is the role of politics simply excluded as a core aspect of war in reality.

NATO's Article Five reflects Clausewitz's dictum that defense "is the stronger form of waging war."[114] Moreover, on the political level, the defense gives a message that emphasizes the link between force, politics, and ideas, as well as mass politics.

The defense being at first passive,[115] NATO's choice of an alliance for the institution's format and the defensive role it played recognized that "war serves the purpose of the defense more than that of the aggressor,"[116] and reflected some of Clausewitz's core principles. Alliances are formed of allies. Allies, according to Clausewitz, represent the "ultimate source of support" as long as these allies have "a *substan-*

---

[111] Clausewitz, *On War*, 77.
[112] Ibid., 579.
[113] NATO, *North Atlantic Treaty*, art 9.
[114] Clausewitz, *On War*, 359.
[115] Ibid., 357–59.
[116] Ibid., 370.

tial interest in maintaining the integrity of their ally's country."[117] Clausewitz's territorial view of defense certainly reinforced the necessity of unity for the European allies, but it does not explain the unconditional engagement of the United States or Canada, as an invasion of any European state would not directly endanger the North American countries. Is the interest of the Alliance really about territorial integrity or about something more in the realm of political imponderables?

The signatory parties not only agreed on an explicit territorial defense in Articles Five and Six, but also on a set of common ideological values to be defended in the introductory paragraph. This approach of defense is reinforced by Article Four, which is also adverse to "political independence or security."[118] Thus, the geography may be relegated to the background of concerns if the threat is more indirect than an armed attack. Ideology by itself is a basis for political decision and thus becomes a "political object—the original motive for the war,"[119] as Clausewitz states. As a threat against the freedom of a distant ally is a threat against a member state's own freedom in the near future, territoriality becomes less relevant than the political symbol under attack. Ideology intertwined with geography blended the "political and military objective"[120] and reinforced the cohesion of the newborn Alliance. This point also explains the unconditional engagement of such faraway allies as the United States and Canada in "a *substantial interest* in maintaining the integrity of their ally's country."[121] This integrity is more than territorial; it is ideological.[122]

---

[117] Clausewitz, *On War*, 373. Although Article Five is binding, it does not generate a fixed and automatized response from the parties. This also reflects the recognition of the difference between war in the abstract and war in reality. Therefore, it gives a chance to the allies to de-conflict frictions before going into action.
[118] NATO, *North Atlantic Treaty*, art 4.
[119] Clausewitz, *On War*, 81.
[120] Ibid.
[121] Ibid., 373.
[122] Thomas, *Promise of Alliance*, 109. Thomas showed the risk of downplaying of ideology during the Détente. Ibid., 57. "Battle for the minds of men."

NATO's Article Nine reflects Clausewitz's spirit within the Alliance's military-political structure (secretary general as well as Supreme Allied Commander Europe (SACEUR), North Atlantic Council (NAC) as well as Military Committee MC, and NAC and Standing Group as above the SACEUR, and so forth), and the consultative process needed to achieve any agreement inside NATO.[123] If diplomacy failed to maintain peace, it would give way to the use of force, and NATO, according to Article Nine, would be acting as a war cabinet, and according to Article Five, as a force. As in democracy, where the statesman is not combined with the soldier in one person, the use of a war cabinet is prescribed by Clausewitz with the emphasis on the "cabinet's participations in military decisions" rather than in political ones.[124] In 1949, the North Atlantic Council (NAC) was comprised of foreign ministers overseeing the Standing Group; later, the Defense Committee (DC) was comprised of defense ministers of the Alliance' nations, answering to their respective head of states, who in turn, would oversee the Military Committee (MC)—chiefs of staff. These committees were derived products from the earlier Anglo-American committees formed in 1941, which made coalition and alliance warfare possible amid problems across the Atlantic and the Pacific oceans and lasted until the end of war.

When comparing NATO's structures to Clausewitz's idea of the political control of the military instrument, one can sees the parallel without difficulty.[125] As Clausewitz puts it, "Unless pure hatred made all wars a struggle for life and death ... no other possibility exists, then, than to subordinate the military point of view to the political."[126] In this spirit, the subordination of the military to the political is done by the NAC when it discusses and implements its respective

---

[123] Thomas, *Promise of Alliance*. Thomas demonstrated that it was not always easy, especially with the Suez Crisis and its aftermath. However, with the Three Wise Men Report, NATO's internal crisis in the Suez's aftermath reinforced the democratic value inside the Alliance.

[124] Clausewitz, *On War*, 608.

[125] Especially if the structural changes are put in relation with the progressive abandonment of the Massive Retaliation concept, which was deemed less and less politically correct as the political and diplomatically structures of NATO grew.

[126] Clausewitz, *On War*, 607.

government's policy in the council. The dialogue between the NAC and the DC avoids the risk for governments to receive only "purely military advice,"[127] which could be detrimental to the conduct of war. Finally, the dialogue between the DC and the MC insures that military plans are not "worked in ignorance of political factors."[128]

From the first structure of NATO in 1949 to that of the Council today, some structural changes have occurred. Those structural changes have enhanced the political[129] and military capacities without impairing the political and diplomatic spheres. The 1967 Harmel Report,[130] which followed "the Three Wise Men Report,"[131] was finalized to enhance the civil-military side effectiveness of the Alliance, despite claims by endless critics to the contrary. Diplomatic and political activities have never stopped, and on the contrary, were expanded during the Cold War period and during any of NATO's military actions, from the 1990s to today. NATO's political and strategic adaptation to the changing face of security in Europe and beyond can be said to embody an understanding of Clausewitz's well-known dictum that "war is merely the continuation of policy by other means."[132] Nonetheless, the integrated military force under centralized command has maintained itself from the down of the atomic era into the post–1989 era.

Critics of the Alliance, who propose a hegemonic structure or focus narrowly on the mission, see the coalition as a means of breaking the bond with the political core of the Alliance and fail to see the vir-

---

[127] Clausewitz, *On War*, 607

[128] Ibid., 608.

[129] Thomas, *Promise of Alliance*, 57. "NATO was urged to become more than a military alliance by turning the Atlantic community 'into a vital and vigorous political reality.'"

[130] NATO, "Future Tasks of the Alliance—'Harmel Report,'" last updated November 14, 2011, http://www.nato.int/cps/en/natolive/80830.htm.

[131] NATO, *The Committee of Three*, 1956, http://www.nato.int/archives/committee_of_three/CT.pdf.

[132] Clausewitz, *On War*, 87. Better defined in his Book Eight, Chapter B: "War is an Instrument of Policy," 605.

tues of the collaborative, political truth in Articles Two, Three, and Four.

The Washington Treaty also relates to Clausewitz's "paradoxical trinity" of the nature of war in fact versus war in theory,[133] that is, in its different levels of war. The Alliance's coordination of ways and means in a combined action reflects democratic statecraft and the realities of pluralistic politics. In its original form, *Chances* are in Articles Three and Five. References to what Clausewitz called *Hatred* may be found in the introductory paragraph and in Articles Two and Four. *Reasons* may be found in Articles One and Nine. The acceptance of the trinity in the foundation text of the Alliance is at the same time the acceptance of the primacy of politics over the military. This attempt to politicize the war, to keep it contained, and avoid an escalation toward its extreme form, proved theoretically possible in Clausewitz's magnum opus and practically possible since Hiroshima.

According to Articles One and Nine of the North Atlantic Treaty, the Alliance rests on the "self-imposed, imperceptible limitations hardly worth mentioning, known as international law and custom,"[134] which gives NATO its structures and processes, thus, its own grammar and the logic for the link to the political and strategic level of war as part of the Alliance. Some can argue that Clausewitz was not advocating for the respect of international law, in which case they would dismiss the idea that NATO was founded Clausewitzian foundations.

But is this the case? In "The Development of NATO EBAO (Effect Based Approach Operation) Doctrine: Clausewitz's Theories and the Role of Law in an Evolving Approach to Operations," Colonel Jody M. Prescott explains how Clausewitz advocated for the respect

---

[133] Clausewitz, *On War*, 89.
[134] Ibid., 75.

of international law in the historical context of his time.[135] The counter-argument would be Operation Allied Force in Kosovo, which started without an explicit United Nations Security Council mandate. Nonetheless, it started with the consent of a large majority of the international community under their responsibility to protect a population and to avoid a new Holocaust. However, the Independent International Commission on Kosovo sees it as justified.[136]

Ryan C. Hendrickson in *Pursuing Strategy*[137] also notes the events that led to such action. By the same token, the tacit accord from the United Nations (UN) after the failure of Rambouillet and the massacre of Racak with the glooming prospect of ethnic cleansing did motivate the strikes under a humanitarian concern in order to avoid a situation as seen in Bosnia years before. In Clausewitz's words, NATO used a certain degree of force that was scaled on its political demand toward Serbia.[138] However, although NATO's air strikes were deemed illegal, the deployment of the Kosovo Forces (KFOR)

---

[135] Colonel Jody M. Prescott, "The Development of NATO EBAO Doctrine: Clausewitz's Theories and the Role of Law in an Evolving Approach to Operations," *Penn State International Law Review* 27, no 1 (Summer 2008), 168. "Because of the very central role that politics play in Clausewitz's ideas, and his appreciation of the significance of political and political-like effects in the non-linear systems that armed conflicts tend to be, it is unnecessary to modify Clausewitz's theories substantially to accommodate the role of law today in either their theoretical or practical aspects. The soundness of Clausewitz's holistic analysis of armed conflict and his appreciation of its non-linear nature make his theories consistent with the theoretical underpinnings of EBAO. His identification of politics as the most important factor in understanding armed conflict allows the modern reader to easily factor the current role of law in military operations into his theories without distorting their conceptual integrity." Ibid.

[136] Independent International Commission on Kosovo, *The Kosovo Report* (2000), http://sitemaker.umich.edu/drwcasebook/files/the_kosovo_report_and_update.pdf. "The Commission concludes that the NATO military intervention was illegal but legitimate. It was illegal because it did not receive prior approval from the United Nations Security Council. However, the Commission considers that the intervention was justified because all diplomatic avenues had been exhausted and because the intervention had the effect of liberating the majority population of Kosovo from a long period of oppression under Serbian rule." Ibid.

[137] Edström and Gyllensporre, *Pursuing Strategy*, 82–93.

[138] Clausewitz, *On War*, 585.

did happen in accordance with the United Nations Security Council Resolution 1244.

C. NATO'S USE OF FORCE (1991–2010)

During the Cold War, the Alliance's goal was to avoid a conflict in Europe, which might have escalated to a nuclear exchange, thus re-enforcing its choice of a defensive alliance, despite criticism that NATO was inherently aggressive. Ultimately, the purpose of this defensive alliance is to compel the adversary to NATO's will.[139] In this respect, the Cold War was won without firing a single shot, in an "armed observation,"[140] through the coordinated use of military ways and means supported by an efficient, coordinated diplomacy and in spite of significant crises. In 1990–1991, with the Kuwait episode, war returned forcefully to the diplomatic system. In Bosnia and Kosovo, NATO imposed its will on its designated adversary in a slow but deliberate process that was also inherently political and which applied limited force to achieve a limited political goal in the western Balkans. NATO used diplomacy as well as military might in a limited manner on the battlefields, which aroused much criticism among strategic fundamentalists and proponents of the operational level as the supreme form of war.

NATO's way of war was not always limited, at least not limited in theory and in the preparation for conflict. In Clausewitz's vocabulary, it tended not only toward the "absolute form of war"[141] but almost to an "extreme: a clash of forces freely operating and obedient to no law but their own."[142] During NATO's first period under Strategic Concept MC 14, a massive nuclear retaliation certainly would have brought the political logic to a stop. In his time, Clausewitz asserted that "war never breaks out wholly unexpectedly, nor can it be spread

---

[139] Clausewitz, *On War*, 75. "War is thus an act of force to compel our enemy to do our will."

[140] Clausewitz, *On War*, 81. "Wars can have all degrees of importance and intensity, ranging from a war of extermination down to a simple armed observation."

[141] Ibid., 582.

[142] Ibid., 78.

instantaneously."[143] But even this proposed policy of massive nuclear retaliation was subject to political limits and the operationalization of the idea in practice required a political adjustment, say, from 1958 onward with the Berlin crisis.

After the Soviet acquisition of nuclear and hydrogen bombs, the notion of limitations of war in the pursuit of minor advantages[144] took on a new value; MC 14/3, known as "Flexible Response," came into effect. Within a time of reduced Cold War tensions that required the Harmel doctrine of the "dual track,"[145] the political counterpart to MC 14/3, became a highly effective approach, employing both security and diplomacy.[146] In NATO's third period, after the Soviet Union collapsed in 1991, NATO revised its concept profoundly to win even more limited war if needed. It was the first time such strategic concepts were openly published, in 1991, 1999, and finally, in 2010.

The view of NATO as a defensive alliance held during the Cold War, but may be questioned in the case of its interventions in the Balkans in the 1990s. Did NATO change its posture fundamentally? Did the change in the strategic concepts divert NATO from its defensive purpose? The answer is no. Following the downfall of the Soviet Union, NATO grew from its 12 original members in 1949, to 16 (from 1982 to 1999), to the 28 current members. This growth shifted the principal focus to security concerns as well as the way to address them. From a conflict where the front lines were fused with the national borders of a neighborhood nation, the focus shifted to how to stabilize a situation that could potentially threaten the Alliance by a proxy conflict.

The Strategic Concept (SC) of 1991 and the following concepts address such threats by enabling security by cooperation, crisis management, and conflict prevention. The SC of 1991 stipulates, "The success of the Alliance's policy of preserving peace and preventing

---

[143] Clausewitz, *On War*, 78.

[144] Ibid., 582.

[145] Thomas, *Promise of Alliance*, 117–21.

[146] Ibid., 90–92. "From peacekeeping to peace making," as observed by Harlan Cleveland in 1967.

war depends even more than in the past on the effectiveness of preventive diplomacy and successful management of crises affecting the security of its members,"[147] which reaffirms Clausewitz.

According to Paragraph 44, "Allies' forces must be adapted to provide capabilities that can contribute to protecting peace, managing crises that affect the security of Alliance members, and preventing war, while retaining at all times the means to defend, if necessary, all Allied territory and to restore peace."[148] In 1991, Bosnia and Kosovo were not in NATO's mind—neither was Afghanistan. The Strategic Concept of 1991 essentially opened the possibility for NATO to intervene if a conflict threatened the security of an allied nation in order to preserve peace. The Strategic Concepts of 1999 and 2010 reinforced it. This gave the opening to an unexpected outcome at that time, which is the corollary to a shift from a territorial threat to NATO to a more diffuse and globalized risk, which the allies addressed under non-article Five basis in Bosnia, Kosovo, Libya, and Afghanistan.[149]

War involves fog and frictions. The Warsaw Pact was generally easier to understand than ethnic conflicts and their ramifications, which would become a new environment after being forgotten for half a century. NATO, during its first 40 years (1949–1989), was not so concerned about fog and frictions, partially because they were present in a lesser degree than today due to the well-known political and geostrategic situation. After the end of the Cold War and with NATO's new role, these factors became more central to NATO's achievements. On the other hand, during the Cold War, NATO was conducting a "war on paper" rather than a "real war" expressed in the physical world.[150]

---

[147] NATO, "The Alliance's New Strategic Concept," (November 8, 1991), para. 31, http://www.nato.int/cps/en/natolive/official_texts_23847.htm.

[148] NATO, "Alliance's New Strategic Concept," para. 44.

[149] For the action taken by NATO in response to the invocation of Article 5, see David S. Yost, *NATO's Balancing Act* (Washington, DC: United States Institute of Peace Press, 2014), 53–54.

[150] Clausewitz, *On War*, 582.

The near absence of friction during NATO's first four decades is thus explainable, as is the larger amount of frictions and fog since the 1990s.[151] In the 1990s, war became again a human activity in which NATO had a role to play. On the material side, NATO tried to minimize possible sources of friction such as the use of standard agreements (STANAG) and implemented recognition of friend-or-foe systems among other choices. On the human side, exercises, training, and lessons learned were used to find and negate as much as possible the role of friction. Today's frictions are less a matter of weather or a problem of night. Newer frictions have developed along with the technological advances that are supposed to eliminate the fog and friction in war. Today, a war without satellite communications is as unbelievable as the use of birds to detect gas attack during the first Gulf War due to the lack of alarm systems to warn the allied troops.

In this regard, operational setbacks in the Balkans, Afghanistan, and Libya can be explained at least partially by inaccurate expectations, overreliance on intelligence, and techniques that led the Alliance to misjudge the "kind of war on which they [were] embarking."[152] Additionally, the Alliance and its political leaders forgot momentarily that war is a "collision of two living forces" that interact in a constant manner.[153] Action means reaction, and in the connected world of today, the reaction may not be localized in the conflict theater but far away, as the audience is now globalized too.[154] Moreover, frictions also result from the Alliance's multi-nationality and multi-cultural format, notwithstanding national interpretations of interests and needs.

These aspects have received exaggerated attention. The advocates of military force over-emphasize the tactical and operational, in the manner of Jomini and others who elevate lower levels of war to strategy. These advocates have constantly criticized the pluralistic forma-

---

[151] A second part of the explanation is the relationships between the level of violence, the emotion of the mass, and the policy. See von Clausewitz, *On War*, 81, 87–88.
[152] Clausewitz, *On War*, 88.
[153] Ibid., 77.
[154] For more on this subject, see Simpson, *War from the Ground Up*.

tion of strategy as betraying timeless verities of war. These critics are, in fact, expecting ill-equipped soldiers within actual war to adjust to the changing realities of conflict.

National frictions in a limited conflict such as the Balkans and Afghanistan are more visible than in a case of the invocation of Article Five. Clausewitz explains it in terms of the need of the political to mobilize the emotion of the masses[155] in an operation with a limited political objective.[156] In other words, frictions will be more visible, with the exception of the Article Five commitment, in which the survival of the Alliance and the way of life of its populations are at stake. Friction's causes are less a matter of technology than a matter of time for negotiations at a strategic level. However, the consensus in the political decision-making process is designed to overcome these frictions but can sometimes create operational setbacks, induced by inaccurate expectations and leading to unexpected outcomes.

D. CONCLUSION

Ultimately, NATO is the exemplification of Clausewitz's idea that "the destruction of the enemy is not the only means of attaining the political object."[157] Therefore, it establishes the primacy of the politics over the military. Since its foundation, NATO has followed Clausewitz's principles, although its principal founding members were not Clausewitzian per se, and some members—like the United States—would take time to embrace a more Clausewitzian approach to the military realm.

---

[155] Clausewitz, *On War*, 88. "If policy is directed only toward minor objectives, the emotions of the masses will be little stirred and they will have to be stimulated rather than held back": The political stirring is a cause of frictions. Such frictions have less chance to occur in a survival situation when article 5 is invoked (in which case it is not anymore a "minor objective").

[156] Ibid., 81. "The less involved the population and the less serious the strains within states and between them, the more political requirements in themselves will dominate … a military objective that matches the political object in scale will, if the latter is reduced, be reduced in proportion."

[157] Clausewitz, *On War*, 95.

The will of a group of democracies to survive through an alliance forced upon its foundation a Clausewitzian approach, which at the time may have not been a sign of will, but of necessity. Despite prior strategic schools of thought, the funding members, when confronted over national interests, came to agree on a Clausewitzian way. It is then not surprising that the North Atlantic Treaty came to exist through a strategic genius for handling of polarity and frictions.

The natural choice of a defensive posture and alliance under international law imposed a respect of values recognized by the diverse trinities of the Alliance and supported by the mass publics at the time and which prevail today. From its first structure, its following evolution, and under the impulse of the Harmel Report, NATO finished strengthening its relation within the trinity by acquiring a subtle parity between Chance, Reason, and Hatred. This subtle equilibrium between the three is the key which supported NATO through the public consciousness, and permitted the survival of the Alliance[158] when the Warsaw Pact died. Having incorporated politics and diplomacy, and accepted being subdued to it, NATO was able through adaptation to outlive the Warsaw Pact in longevity.

NATO, by its construct and history, was and still is able to handle the whole spectrum of violence, in Clausewitz's words from a "mere armed observation" to a literal "annihilation's war."[159] Today, NATO has the means to handle limited conflict but is, at the same time, ready for the full spectrum. However, if NATO can compel and deter, the transition from military operations to a civil authority has, in every operation, demonstrated that NATO cannot and will not rule over the political realm and will stay subordinate to the political. If NATO is the surrogate for war, then it fulfills Clausewitz's concept of war as "merely the continuation of policy by other means."[160]

---

[158] Thomas, *Promise of Alliance*, 58. As foreseen by Secretary of State Herter in 1957 and expressed by Thomas, "NATO could outlive the Soviet threat" by adaptation when facing an internal crisis.

[159] Clausewitz, *On War*, 81: "War can have all degrees of importance and intensity, ranging from a war of extermination down to a simple armed observation."

[160] Ibid., 87.

IV. EFFECTS AND CONSEQUENCES OF CLAUSEWITZ ON COUNTERINSURGENCY

In the last two decades since the early 1990s, terrorism and insurgency have formed an undeniable link. Terrorism acts in two ways; the first is as an external factor to the main theater of operation. Its purpose is age old: to exercise some level of terror in the other camp and to exhaust the opponent's will to pursue its action by exercising pressure on the people who are not directly in the combat zone.

The second part of terrorism acts as a logistical base to recruit new insurgents for the theater of operations and to provide support for the "front." The increase of terrorists in the theater of operations leads to a growth of the insurgency, which in turn tips the equilibrium of violence toward escalation. The logical tactical response is to escalate toward COIN operations. Terrorism and COIN operations are linked by the political realm, thus implying a coordination of the political with the military that, through a whole governmental approach, may resolve the root of the problem. Thus, it demands a top-down strategy.

A. SHIFTS IN THE TERRORIST REALM

The problem, for counterterrorism, with today's terrorist organizations is that they are not as organized as before, like the West German Red Faction Army of the 1970s, for example. Today, there is no network, at least not in the traditional conception. For example, there is no real chain of command, but only an idea on which terrorists act. To some extent, this new form of terrorism represents the absolute form of the "Auftragstaktik" with its absence of a direct command and control (C2) network. It is an independent cell, sometimes composed of a single actor, with no logistic ties and no indoctrination sessions. The new terrorists radicalize themselves alone via the Internet or while in jail, and then decide one day, without warning or orders, to act. They may regroup, but this is an exception, not a trend. Most of the time, they do not even know that other potential "terrorists" are near them. Some join fighting groups abroad and then will be dealt with as an insurgency. For those who stay in a country to act, they are seen as "stay behind"[161] actors; they are lone actors who have to be dealt with through judicial action.

Through their way of life and experiences with society, they find a new purpose in their life. Whether they live in jail or die for Islam, they are "martyr-heroes" in their own view in both worlds (paradise or jail). It is not a classical political combat in which terrorism was a necessity and a last action to help the cause. Today the political fight is replaced by religious dogma; this religious dogma is another form of policy—it is a religious fight for the supremacy of a faith, idealized or not. Killing terrorists, like killing insurgents, only helps fuel the myth by creating new martyrs, like the Christians in the past when Rome tried to eradicate them.[162]

B. THE LINKAGE BETWEEN TODAY TERRORISM AND THE TRINITY

Carl Schmitt remarked in *The Concept of the Political* that "a world in which the possibility of war is utterly eliminated, a completely pacified globe, would be a world without the distinction of friend and enemy and hence a world without politics."[163] Like Clausewitz, Schmitt recognized that polarization created by politics is the fuel for violence and war. Politics should not be understood in narrow terms of left or right; politics are to be understood as a result of a human action toward a goal. Schmitt continued that "the justification of war does not reside in its being fought for ideals or norms of justice, but in its being fought against a real enemy,"[164] which enemy is a threat to one's way of life.[165] Insurgency is an act of last resort for a segment of soci-

---

[161] Although there is no organizational structure as there was for the "Stay Behind" from the Cold War era, the underlying idea and use of such elements is the same. Due to the lack of C2, it will be difficult to estimate how many they are, search for them, and destroy their capabilities.

[162] Romain Grand (Geneva Police Officer), Skype discussion with the author, January 23, 2015.

[163] Carl Schmitt, *The Concept of the Political* (Chicago: University of Chicago Press, 2007), 35.

[164] Schmitt, *Concept of Political*, 49.

[165] Ibid.

ety to assert its differences in order to survive and to avoid that "decision to be made by another, [because] then it is no longer a politically free people and is absorbed into another political system"[166] in which "it ceases to exist politically."[167]

Clausewitz also come to this conclusion "with the retreat of the army into the interior—no matter how complete the defeat of a state—the potential of fortresses and general insurrections must be evoked."[168] Thus, insurgency is first a political act of survival expressed through fighting for its own way of life. Therefore, when a regime change is the military goal of a policy leading to a war, insurgency has to be taken seriously in the military planning, because it will, with high probability, arise.

Hannah Arendt remarks in *On Violence* that "the emergence of a new society was preceded, but not caused, by violent outbreaks."[169] In other words, the causes of violence are grievances. Thus, independent of whether the regime change comes from an external actor, as in Iraq or Afghanistan, or internally, as seen in multiple revolutions, it is followed by counterrevolution, leading to change. As the means is insurgency, the end is the choice of one's way of life, and the way is a political struggle. The assumptions of the relevance of the trinity—chance, hatred, reason—survives. Consequently, the survival of the trinity led Clausewitz to "consider general insurrection as simply another means of war."[170] That is, the insurrection or insurgency is generally not a matter of numbers; the roots of the insurgency are still the same. However, the military capacity is restrained to counterbalance the mean of fighting chosen by the adversary. Both the way and end of the adversary are out of reach of armies' might.

When in the middle of engaging with an insurgency, the missing link is to adapt Clausewitz principles. It is still a duel of will in relation to an enemy; however, instead of the clash of two trinities in this trial,

---

[166] Schmitt, *Concept of Political*, 49.
[167] Ibid.
[168] Clausewitz, *On War*, 483.
[169] Hannah Arendt, *On Violence* (New York: A Harvest Book Harcourt, 1970), 11.
[170] Clausewitz, *On War*, 479.

it is the clash of at least three trinities—the one who intervenes, the host nation, and the insurgency's trinity—that clash altogether. To "win the hearts and minds" is to ensure that both the trinity of the intervening and the host nation are in synch against the insurgency. If there is already a discrepancy before, the outcome may not be a good one.

For a third party caught in a host nation's insurgency, the question is then how to influence the basic trinity (Figure 3) for each party when they are juxtaposed philosophically (Figure 4), and to shift the center of gravity, the population (c), which represents the hearts and minds to be won (Figure 5)? There are few solutions other than an overlapping of the trinities of the host nation with the one of the third party.

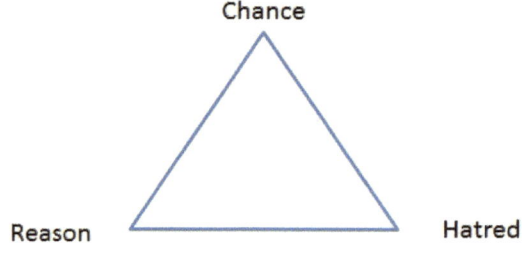

Figure 3, Basic Trinity of an Involved Party

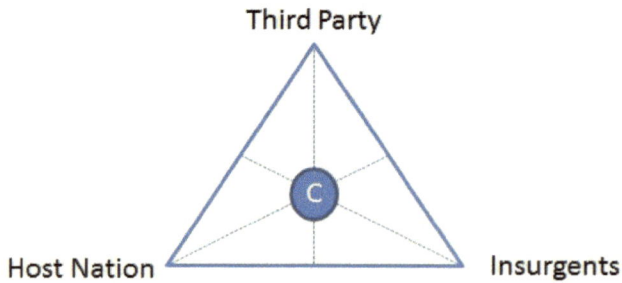

Figure 4, Trinities' Interrelationship

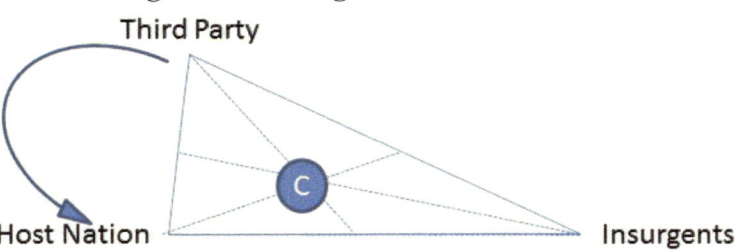

Figure 5, Winning "Hearts and Minds"

Even if done successfully, a fraction of the population (red) will still be unconditionally insurgents per se (see Figure 6), but the majority represented by the unconditional supporter of the host nation (green) and the "bystanders" (blue) will be receptive to change for a certain period of time. This window of opportunity should then be exploited to the host nation's advantage.

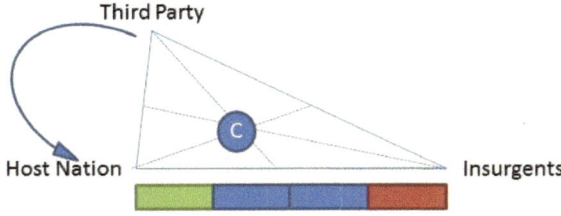

Figure 6, Population Support Model

C. A POSSIBLE TRINITARIAN APPROACH TO INSURGENCY

In order to counterbalance the insurgency and its mean of fighting, one has to examine Clausewitz's Book VI and his comment on the use of insurrection as a part of a war plan. However, it can be used in the context of insurgency as the rules will be the same. Clausewitz remarks that insurgencies are the result "of the breaking down of barriers."[171] Those barriers were the medieval estates in the face of the French Revolution and the decline of absolutism in the eighteenth century. The democratization of armed forces led the mass of people to put their hands on weapons and learn to use them, which in turn led to people's war under Napoleon. Today, the democratization of forces and the availability of weapons continues apace. As Clausewitz remarks, such resources in war are somewhat limited, especially in insurgency, thus they have to be used intelligently to achieve a psychological effect.[172] In insurgency, "by its very nature, such scattered resistance will not lend itself to major actions, closely compressed in time and space."[173] This statement is worth analyzing more closely.

First, the adversary is scattered, which does not allow it to use mass. Second, resistance is a form of defense, according to Clausewitz a superior form in relation to the offense. Third, because the mass is denied to the insurgency, the insurgents do not have the capacity to either hit hard or decisively, repetitively, in a short time or over long distance; this is why time is working for them and against the occupant.

To at least reduce insurgency in the military form, the scattering effect of the resistance should be augmented. This augmentation has to be done by the use of the mass on the side of occupying force, however, without a concentration of mass, which would present an optimal target to the resistance. This point is an argument against separate military bases and compounds and rather for more small outposts in large numbers in the populated area.

If the resistance is superior because on a defense posture, the resistance has to be provoked into offense. But in doing so, undue casualties in the population should be avoided.

By denying the resistance of the mass of the population and by forcing them into action, the insurgents will have to expose themselves to achieve a result or disappear in order to avoid extinction. However, the goal at the operational level of war is to destroy the

---

[171] Clausewitz, *On War*, 479.
[172] Ibid.
[173] Ibid., 480.

resistance, not to let it slip away. Therefore, the use of deception has to be enhanced to give the insurgents a reason to regroup in the hope of hitting the target of their choice hard and decisively in a single point; if successful, such a scheme can destroy the resistance, but it has to be credible, like Patton's army in England. The other option is to disperse the resistance in such an area that it is virtually impossible for its members to regroup for long enough that the movement eventually dies by inaction.

Clausewitz does not see a great difference in insurgency between a poor population or a richer one. However, in this case, we have to remember that force, at a strategic and operational level of war, has two components, physical and moral. The way to act on physical force will be the same, but the resilience of the moral force may differ greatly enough that a tactic used on a poor population may not work on a richer one, or the reverse. Nonetheless, the moral force in insurgency is a key factor. Clausewitz pointed it out, and General Tony Zinni experienced it firsthand in Vietnam as he recalled, "to counter insurgents, we needed people's courage, commitment, and rejection of the enemy,"[174] while on the side of the insurgents, they needed "fear, apathy, or support. Any of these would do."[175] Fear can be addressed by the occupation forces by providing security; however, apathy or support for the insurgency will primarily be resolved by the political outcome, which is out of the hands of the armed forces; the people must go from being bystanders to becoming stakeholders. Zinni's point is that the supported government has to "meet their [the people] needs."[176]

Clausewitz is definite, however, on the use of such insurgents, not "against the main enemy force or … any sizable enemy force."[177] There is a correct ratio between the size of the occupation forces and the potential threat to be found which can lead to an effective force protection and the security of the population. The use of insurgents

---

[174] Tony Zinni and Tony Koltz, *Before the First Shots Are Fired: How America Can Win or Lose Off the Battlefield* (New York: Palgrave MacMillan, 2014), 5.
[175] Ibid.
[176] Ibid., 6.
[177] Clausewitz, *On War*, 480.

may be predicted "to nibble at the shell and around the edges."[178] Therefore, the disposition has to be such that there is no edge in the military operation, but just a hard shell. This requires mass on the side of the occupant, dispersed in such a way that all potential targets are shell and work as a denial of area. As Clausewitz remarks, "the people who have not yet been conquered by the enemy will be the most eager to arm against him."[179] If true, this fact implies that the occupying force should rapidly and massively occupy the convoyed territory to avoid the possibility that a resistance/insurgence can develop. The mass and the speed at which the occupation develop also have a psychological effect. However, contrary to the Shock and Awe strategy, the emphasis is more on mass than speed. At the moment the occupation starts, it marks the inflection point on the continuum of violence. This point is also the moment where mass and speed no longer have the same signification for the invader. Earlier, during Phase III, speed is the main factor, supported by a lesser mass. After this point, mass is the main factor, supported by speed. In the case of Iraq, this point was the end of combat operations against the Iraqi army, the end of the "symmetrical" fight. If the transition occurs in a timely way, it should delay or avoid what Clausewitz called the propagation of the flames of insurrection.[180] In other word, counterinsurgency should be seen as a succession of operations going from containment to attrition, as Clausewitz argues that insurgents "should not be allowed to go to pieces through too many men being killed, wounded or taken prisoner: such defeats would soon dampen its ardor."[181]

Finally, fighting leads to annihilation of the armed resistance. That is, by denying the relationship between regular troops and insurgents coupled with the denial of safe haven for regrouping, training, and organization through massive occupation, the lid would been kept on the boiling pot. For Vietnam and Afghanistan, the safe havens were North Vietnam[182] and Pakistan, respectively. For Iraq, it may have

---

[178] Clausewitz, *On War*, 480–81.
[179] Ibid., 481.
[180] Ibid.
[181] Clausewitz, *On War*, 482.
[182] Zinni and Koltz, *Before First Shots Are Fired*, 8.

been Syria or some patch of desert. In such a theater of operation, the insurgency is no longer able to use fear as a weapon to "arouse uneasiness and fear,"[183] or as a recruitment tool.

The goal is to deny the insurgency the capacity to build up enough forces to challenge the occupant in symmetrical fighting, for it is the only way to defeat a state. Now, containment, attrition, and annihilation are not necessarily linear tasks. In this respect, Clear–Hold–Build makes perfect sense in a military tactical view, but to be efficient it cannot be linear and certainly not only tactical. Zinni expressed the same for another time: "Vietnam was a simultaneous war, not a sequential one."[184] If the military operation can take care of the armed insurgency, military units are not able to address the two other constituencies of the insurgency: the *end*, which is the choice of one's way of life, and the *way*, which is the political struggle. In Zinni's words, "the 'whole of government' must be committed;"[185] however, the reality in the case of Iraq and Afghanistan was otherwise.[186] Armed forces can solve the part relative to the "physical force," but as Clausewitz pointed out, there are also "moral forces" to be taken care of.

Insurgents can only challenge the occupying force in a symmetrical fashion if they have the support of regular troops. That is why it is vital to maintain regular troops under one's command once they have been subdued. In the case of Iraq, as seen, the disbandment was a major error. The cleaning of the Iraqis' ranks could have been done with time in an orderly fashion enclosed in a judicial process led by the host nation. Former enemies who were loyal servants to the host nation may have been pardoned under conditions which allowed a better future for all. Alas, what happened in Iraq just fueled the insurgency side.

This fact also shows that the inflection point discussed before also represents the moment in which the political leadership should retake the lead of operations. The way of life for which an adversary fights is

---

[183] Clausewitz, *On War*, 482.
[184] Zinni and Koltz, *Before First Shots Are Fired*, 7.
[185] Ibid., 106.
[186] Ibid., 106–107.

directly linked to his political view of his world. Therefore, in order to sustain military operations crushing the armed part of the insurgency, the political level has to coordinate how to settle the roots of the problems that have led to the insurgency in parallel to the military action.[187] This step can only be done by a profound understanding of the adversary's trinity in his own narrative and certainly not in the "occupant" narrative. With slight interpretational differences, the Clausewitzian approach could still work if it is broken down to a single unit. However, terrorists are not a military problem but a judicial one.

The challenges lie in intelligence and coordination between the frontline in which the armies collect intelligence and the fusion with the rear, back in the countries subject to terrorism. It is a "whole government approach" which has to be efficiently coordinated. What changed is not war, but the way the adversary prepares itself in an intrastate conflict. Thus, counterinsurgency is a national-level undertaking, as remarked by Captain Brett Friedmann, because counterinsurgency is linked to the adversary trinity and military means are good at tactical victories, but only a sound political strategy can transform tactical victories into strategic victories, hence, peace. As consequences, first, an insurgency is not a special case of war, it is just another expression of it along the continuum of violence. Second, the trinity is still the central element. Third, there is no military solution alone as the issue is rooted in politics.

The first consequence affects armies on the planning level to avoid a vacuum of security, which gives the essential condition for an insurgency. At the doctrinal level, provisions for the education and training of troops to conduct such tasks have to be made. As discussed earlier in this paper, the choice of troops and equipment is relevant to conduct counterinsurgency, which affects the procurement level.

The second consequence affects first and foremost the framing of the problem and intelligence. Decoding the adversary trinity in its own environment requires more than data collection, and it is time-

---

[187] Gen Karl W. Eikenberry on Afghanistan in Zinni and Koltz, *Before First Shots Are Fired*, 5.

consuming. In turn, the result will certainly impact planning, education and training, and procurement.

The third consequence directly affects the strategic level. Once combat operations are finished, the mindset is not war but police action. However, battles may still be fought. This is the "three bloc war" of General Krulak. Nevertheless, the precondition to start Phase IV on good footing has to be established all along the operation lines. As previously stated, the use of force is not contrary to the use of the intellect. If there is an imperative necessity to destroy a target to achieve a military aim at one advantage, let it be. However, the information has to follow the line and feed the process to allow a rapid rebuilding once hostilities end to avoid this vacuum of security. This is not a linear thinking, but nested thinking which necessitates the support of all government agencies.

During a speech delivered to the Association of the United States Army on October 10, 2007, in Washington, DC, Secretary of Defense Robert Gates stated:

> It is hard to conceive of any country challenging the United States directly on the ground--at least for some years to come. Indeed, history shows us that smaller, irregular forces—insurgents, guerrillas, terrorists—have for centuries found ways to harass and frustrate larger, regular armies and sow chaos. ... We can expect that asymmetric warfare [insurgency war] will remain the mainstay of the contemporary battlefield for some time.[188]

He not only remembers well American history—and how the revolutionary war was fought against the British army—but also that "it had happened at least once each generation, and rarely by design."[189] The United States Army of today cannot be defeated by smaller countries with regular means, thus, insurgency war is the most likely to be fought.

If war is approached according to Clausewitz's views, there is a rationale to explain Iraq and Afghanistan not as failures, but as continuity in the efforts of nations to reach national aims. This suggestion

---

[188] Robert Gates cited in Kaplan, *Insurgents*, 277.
[189] Kaplan, *Insurgents*, 365.

not only implies that war is a continuity of policies and not a failure of it, but also that war is a medium to bring people to the negotiation table, not to achieve such an ultimate, total victory as seen during WWII. The Western psyche is biased by its own history. WWII was certainly the most absolute war, but the memory of it diverges from reality. As absolute at it was, it is still an exception in history in terms of scale, purpose, and means. War in Iraq and Afghanistan or in other countries today are rather more typical limited wars, in scopes and goals.

This limitation of war is the counterargument to Bacevich's view to imply the "home front" in the war effort. However, Bacevich, in the author's view, still has a good argument concerning the need of a good relationship between a nation's army and its population base on more than the minimal demonstration of gratitude; for the reasons described by Bacevich, in the long term, an all-voluntary force may not be the optimal solution. If war is seen as a failure of policies, the risks are that war will be longer and costlier than before, as their goals will be formed outside the political realm with the risk of extending their missions. Wars occur as part of human activity; the natural course of human history is not characterized by just war or peace because neither lasts long. Peace can just define a period of time between two wars. People in America have been at peace for a long time, but America has been at war every generation since 1776.

Clausewitz remarks that "envy, jealousy, anxiety and sometime perhaps even generosity are the natural advocates of the unsuccessful."[190] This may summarize the downfall of democratic societies— envy to promulgate their set of valor, jealous of their exceptionalism, anxious of their past which triggers their conscience to share its goods with all.

Shock and Awe is only Jomini's operational half-measure; to achieve a total military victory, one needs Clausewitz's strategic political victory. War is started and finished by the political decision-maker, but wedged by its army. There are efforts to achieve victory: "This effort must not only be made, but be sustained like the upkeep of a

---

[190] Clausewitz, *On War*, 597.

great household."[191] Victory is not only defined by defeating the adversary army, but by its recognition by a sustainable peace treaty: "war and peace admit no gradations."[192] However, Simpson observes rightfully that "to define victory, or success, in one's own terms ... is generally impossible."[193]

Such treaties are necessary, but they were not seen in Afghanistan or Iraq in a recognizable form. Karl Marlantes, in his book *What It Is Like to Go to War,* makes a case for ceremonies, like surrenders or victories, to help consolidate narratives and reduce wounds. No such thing was done and broadcasted at the time in a discernable manner in the United States, save the odd image of President Bush in his flight suit on the deck of an aircraft carrier just as the actual conflict was setting in, despite all "shock and awe." The absence of visible milestones permitted a biased narrative to survive and expand, creating a new problem on top of the older one. DOD Directive 3000.05 which recognized the necessity to "perform all stability lines of operation as 'core mission'" was recognition that a lasting peace is also part of the military operation because it is the aim of all war to reach a better peace.

The conflicts of the last two decades found their inceptions in a Clausewitzian world; it put adversaries that were not abstract at all against one another, and the wars were neither unexpected nor instantaneous.[194] They developed upon mobilization of resources and did not consist of "a single short blow,"[195] and intelligence, although more efficient than before, was still imperfect and sometime inaccurate, which maintained the fog of war[196] on operations despite the technological promises of RMA and network-centric warfare. The Iraq and the Afghanistan invasions were thought and fought in a Clausewitzian framework but in a Jominian way of war.

---

[191] Clausewitz, *On War*, 598.
[192] Ibid., 603.
[193] Simpson, *War from the Ground Up*, 207.
[194] Clausewitz, *On War*, 78.
[195] Ibid., 79.
[196] Ibid., 117.

The seizure of countries was a necessity to achieve the political aim, which was a regime change, but those countries were not to be retained as a prize.[197] This was done after "wear[ing] down the enemy" by containment, which brought Sadam Hussein or the Taliban to a "gradual exhaustion of his physical and moral resistance"[198] and by a short phase of attrition in which the enemy's suffering was increased[199] with the help of Shock and Awe. The Iraqi army was "coerced" and "put in a situation that is even more unpleasant than the sacrifice ... call on [it]":[200] the unpleasant situation at this point was to die for nothing, versus the sacrifice of surrender and stopping hostilities. In this respect, maximum violence used with the "simultaneous use of intellect"[201] effectively renders "war between civilized nations ... far less cruel and destructive"[202] than what was coming during the sectarian violence. The Taliban followed almost the same trajectory as the coalition. From Phase 0, or "shaping the theater," to the end of Phase III, or "dominating activities," the conflict was Clausewitzian; *On War* was applied, if not directly, at least in spirit, up to the occupation.

Then, at the moment when effective political influence regained its influence over military operations, one forgot that even if the occupation is completed, "hostilities can be renewed again in the interior."[203] The research of the causes and distribution of blame regarding Afghanistan and the Iraq War grew in the fertile soil of literature on Afghanistan and the Iraq War in the mid-2000s. However, the answers were in *On War*; the military leadership did read it and mostly understood it, and applied it, as proven by the rapid success of military operations. The political leadership, however, did not heed the advice of the military leadership. The failure, resulting in protracted

---

[197] Clausewitz, *On War*, 93.
[198] Ibid.
[199] Ibid.
[200] Ibid., 77.
[201] Ibid., 75.
[202] Ibid., 76.
[203] Ibid., 90.

conflicts, is to be seen at the junction of the military-strategy level and the political leadership,[204] not by the troops.

---

[204] Daniel Bolger, *Why We Lost: A General's Inside Account of the Iraq and Afghanistan Wars* (Boston: Houghton Mifflin Harcourt, 2014), xv.

V. OLD NEW WARS AND THE ENDURING RELEVANCE OF CLAUSEWITZ

After the 1990s, Clausewitz was widely read in all U.S. military schools and studied to some degree by all branches of the U.S. armed forces. He was read, but he may not have been learned in the manner that the needs of policy, strategy, and operations can be said to have required in the time since. As of the year 2015, first-hand accounts of the Afghanistan and Iraq wars are published and discussed, and generalizations about this literature are urgent for their meaning in the wider body of strategic theory, including its classical part.

This chapter intends to follow *On War*'s layout and to compare and contrast Clausewitz's magnum opus with today's accounts of the recent conflicts in Iraq and Afghanistan. This chapter argues against Dr. Tony Corn, who, in the vein of van Creveld and Liddell Hart before him, states in the tendentious manner that fits the world since 2001, "It is fair to say that Clausewitz's *On War* has never been less relevant as today."[205] In fact, the contrary is truer: Clausewitz is more relevant today than ever before and still misused in U.S. military thinking and practice.

A. ON THE NATURE OF WAR

In his introduction, Clausewitz warns his reader that war is a complex matter, thus, "the part[s] and the whole must always be thought of together."[206] The *parts* of the war go from the soldier in the trench line to the commander-in-chief in his headquarters, including all components of armed forces in the theater that keep them combat-ready such as logistics or intelligence, C2, and elements that may be located far away from the battlefield. The *whole* is as much the physical adversary as the rest of the world, which may have any influence on the war, even if remote in distance or probability.

In the introduction of his article, "Clausewitz in America Today," Christopher Bassford states, in a quote more or less inspired by Field Marshall Helmut von Moltke, "The traditional attitude of American

---

[205] Corn, "From Mars to Minerva," 22.
[206] Clausewitz, *On War*, 75.

soldiers was that 'politics and strategy are radically and fundamentally things apart. Strategy begins where politics end.'"[207] This sentiment was famously also quoted by Douglas MacArthur. Bassford cites the *Principles of Strategy for an Independent Corps or Army in a Theater of Operations*, edited in 1936. In the conclusion of the same article, Bassford cites Colin S. Gray from *The Making of Strategy: Rules, States and War*, in which the latter assesses some characteristics of the American strategic culture highly pertinent not only to the past but also to the record since September 11, 2001: "indifference to history, engineering style and dogged pursuit of technical fix, impatience, blindness to cultural differences, indifference to strategy, and the evasion of politics."[208] Fifty-eight years have elapsed between these quotations; the philosophical gap seems to be even more pronounced.

The conflicts in the two last decades have shown conclusively that history plays a role in the formulation of strategy; technology cannot fix everything, although it may help to save lives and to span geography; impatience by civilians and soldiers within other culture tends to be counterproductive; and finally, that strategy influences politics as much as the reverse: "To see the military as a politically inert executor of policy in a one-way system is to misread Clausewitz."[209] "Politically inert" does not mean apolitical. "Apolitical" means that the Army is neither playing politics for its own sake, nor defying politicians in their core sphere of influence. Apoliticism has to be seen as a translation of the consequence of the military action into a political damage assessment type of service. If the army does Q, the consequences in the political landscape are x, y, and z.

When seen from the perspective of the year 2015, the first influential mainstream text or manifesto against Clausewitz appeared in 1991, Martin van Creveld's *The Transformation of War*.[210] Van Creveld's

---

[207] Quoted in Christopher Bassford, "Clausewitz in America Today," in *Clausewitz Goes Global: Carl von Clausewitz in the 21st Century* [Commemorating the 50th Anniversary of the Clausewitz Society], ed. Clausewitz Gesellschaft and Reiner Pommerin (Berlin: Carola Hartmann Miles Verlag, 2011), 343.

[208] Quoted in Bassford, "Clausewitz in America Today," 352.

[209] Simpson, *War from the Ground Up*, 112.

[210] van Creveld, *Transformation of War*.

position then, almost a generation ago, had some merit, but for reasons pending adequate analysis, the idea of Clausewitz's irrelevance became a dogma. Given whatever context in politics and government, not the least because of the personality of its author, *Transformation of War* was fated to influence military thoughts for almost two decade.

This influence arose as conflict in this period diverged from that of memory and doctrine on a wide scale, especially so after the second Iraqi campaign of 2003 at which time the disconnection between means and ends became fateful for the makers of U.S. strategy. This approach resulted in two main consequences for Western strategy. The first was the tendency by those in charge to see counterinsurgency as a new and separate kind of war; the second was to separate even more the military realm from the political realm, creating a vacuum at a strategic level that precipitated a series of blunders. Everyone today, reading newspapers or books or watching analysis on television, may develop, like van Creveld, the impression that since the events of September 11, war has changed in its most essential character of violence and strategic purpose. But can the nature of war change? If yes, at least one of the factors in Clausewitz's trinity—organized violence, chance, and political effect—must change. The following analysis will test the validity of Clausewitz's assertion of the constancy of war's characteristics as described in *On War*.

Clausewitz opened *On War* with his inquiry into the nature of war and, according to him, "War is thus an act of force to compel our enemy to do our will."[211] Armies still oppose adversaries in the theater of operations and, with the help of force, incapacitate their opponents. As before, the force "equips itself with the inventions of art and science."[212] But there is more at issue than the shiniest, newest technology. Jomini, in the *Art of War*, validates Clausewitz's definition regarding the lack of impact of technology on the nature of war, that "these principles are immutable, independent of types of weapons, time, and country."[213] In other words, an incidental change at

---

[211] Clausewitz, *On War*, 75.
[212] Ibid.
[213] Cited in Simpson, *War from the Ground Up*, 135.

the tactical level does not change the nature of war at the strategic level.

Despite all assertions by grand tacticians to the contrary, those military forces are still ruled by "self-imposed, imperceptible limitations hardly worth mentioning, known as international law and custom, but they scarcely weaken it [the military force]."[214] As did the Greek poet Homer through his hero, Odysseus, with Bie and Metis,[215] Clausewitz divided military force into two distinct parts: the physical aspect and the aspect of moral. During the transition from industrial war in the total age to its nuclear and thermo-nuclear chapters, these two distinct parts, physicality and moral, were replaced by a new dogma of technological primacy at the expense of chance, political purpose, and aspects of anger and hatred as a force of real war.

The Revolution of Military Affairs (RMA), a 1990s invention of defense thinkers and defense contractors with little regard for actual war, took the field with a dominance of rhetoric that did not accord with political realities. Regarding the physical force within the military, ever more strategic idealists argued that since the beginning of the 1990s, the RMA had led to drastic changes in the art of war, leading to changes in strategy in favor of the United States and its high-tech armed forces that could limit the nature of war to exceed its limits with tactical finesse. The armed forces undergoing the RMA were also joining to prove that Jomini's principles were even more contemporary than before, that is, the capacity to mass overwhelming force at the decisive point, ideally interior lines, which now could be subjected

---

[214] Clausewitz, On War, 75.

[215] Freedman, Strategy, 42. The best found description of Bie and Metis is from Edward Hugh in "Metis, Bie and Kerdos: Some Thoughts on Defeating Terrorism," A Fistful of Euros: A European Opinion (Blog), March 13, 2004, http://fistfulofeuros.net/afoe/metis-bie-and-kerdos-some-thoughts-on-defeating-terrorism/. Metis is associated with a particular form of intelligence cunning: "Metis is a type of intelligence and of thought, a way of knowing; it implies a complex but coherent body of mental attitudes and intellectual behavior which combine flair, forethought, resourcefulness, vigilance, pragmatism, opportunism and the wisdom of experience. When art and science unite, extra possibilities and opportunities are made resulting in innovation that can be driven by creativity. Metis is about finding elegant solutions to difficult problems instead of relying on brute force [Bie]."

to a single dominant will in battle in a "system of battles," as it came to be called.

The information revolution would render through new technologies "'near-simultaneous operations.' ... The emphasis would now be on speed, not mass."[216] Speed, not mass, as criteria is valid for certain kinds of combat, weapons, and tactics, but limited to a specific part of the war, known as Phase III. (Phase III relates to the physical destruction of the enemy forces, what came grossly to be described as "kinetic effects.") Conversely, when it comes to stabilization in an area of conflict in which all-out force is unwarranted, the importance of these factors, mass and speed, are reversed. The RMA improved efficiency at the tactical level or appeared to do so, and between the tactical and operational level; however, it did not integrate it with the strategic-political decision-making process. This problem grew more exaggerated as the political strategic level became murky, and the disjuncture of ends and means grew more aggravated in the face of actual events, as in the 1990s, and especially after September 11.

RMA, as useful as it was, only focused on a part of war, and by the emphasis put on it, planners forgot the whole of the war within the poles of violence, chance, and political effect, as well as anger and hatred. Therefore, a critic can well say that the RMA signified nothing more than evolution of ballistic accuracy as well as communications—an adaptation of armies to new technologies of the present information revolution in capitalism and communications, not a revolution nor a new strategy in the longer record of war in the western world. The physical force available to compel an opponent is today greater, stronger, and mightier than ever before, but armies are still influenced by two main factors, speed and mass, just as they were in Clausewitz's time.[217]

Mass and speed are relative factors and do not mean the same for a platoon leader or for a commander-in-chief, neither do they mean the same at a strategical or tactical level, or in the combat phase or in the stabilization phase. The factors speed and mass develop a different meaning depending on the phase of the war. The same is true

---

[216] Kaplan, *Insurgents*, 51.
[217] Clausewitz, *On War*, 617.

when Clausewitz argued to "act with the utmost speed."[218] Once operations start, the utmost speed is certainly needed to exploit surprise; the practice of Shock and Awe of air and land strikes is born out of this idea.

But speed can also be detrimental and lead armed forces to rely on assumptions more than facts. "The slower the progress and the more frequent the interruptions of military action the easier it is to retrieve a mistake, the bolder will be the general's assessments."[219] To "act with the utmost concentration"[220] does not mean the same at the tactical or strategic level. Mass is not only a relative factor, but also has a relative value. A mass of old T-72 armored vehicles does not equal the same number of M1-A1 Abrams tanks; however, both represent a mass to achieve a tactical or operational goal.

The same can be said for Jomini and his principles of war. Simpson, a veteran of contemporary war and a theorist in the classical school, argues that Jomini's principles of war are valid only within a conventional high-intensity conflict.[221] This author argues that it depends on how we look at it. Concentration of forces for example, is relative. Even terrorist have exerted a "concentration of force" in space and time to achieve a goal, as on September 11, 2001. This "concentration of force" can be very limited from an army perspective, but still comparative to the means of the adversary as a concentration of force. Every principle can be seen through the lens of a smaller force and still be applied in combat. The scope may not be what we expect as a military unit.

On the side of the moral force, Clausewitz anchored those in the state and its attributes "for moral force has no existence save as expressed in the state and the law."[222] Today, with ideological conflicts of small violence that are intended to wear down moral and morale, moral force is much more important in the overall strategy of a state

---

[218] Clausewitz, *On War*, 617.
[219] Ibid., 85.
[220] Ibid., 617.
[221] Simpson, *War from the Ground Up*, 136–37.
[222] Clausewitz, *On War*, 75.

at war than before, because of the highly ideological nature of conflict, which might have been less so, say, in the epoch of the wars of the cabinets after 1648 until 1789. Today, states are bound to treaties, moral of actions are discussed on the public realm, and the result of those discussions influences more than before the strategy of a state and its willingness or capacities to implement his military options.

This is the question of the "just war" that has occupied a lot of thinkers in the Western states lately. But for Clausewitz, when he talks about force, meant physical force as the principal means of war but through *On War*, he pays close attention to the morale (which include moral) element as a whole, with his attention to the transformation from dynastic Europe to the Europe of nation-states. Today, the moral element is more prominent because of the codex of the Islamist fighter in conflict with globalized American capitalism in debate, and its influence is greater due to the connectivity of the world, phenomena that Clausewitz did not experience on the same scale, though Clausewitz was well aware of revolutionary ideology and its impact on the traditional state. Speed and mass are not only factors for physical force, they also influence the moral force; who came out with the message first, how quickly can this message be spread (speed), to how many people will the adversary give his one message (mass)? Such factors are relevant to all sides to establish a narrative and mobilize masses to influence opinions. The "near-simultaneous" possibility of influence through mass media has reached a new high with cellphones, for example, rending more difficult the use of force.

The true goal of war, once declared, is not to avoid bloodshed but to render the enemy powerless.[223] This end is achieved by the use of force. In Clausewitz's time, force was generally equated with military might. Today we could extend those forces to diplomatic, economic, and informational, along with military force (DIME). Their activities can therefore cover so-called kinetic and non-kinetic options. One, such as the British critic in the age of total war, Basil Liddell Hart, argued that Clausewitz advocated extremes of force and mass, however "the maximum use of force is in no way incompatible with the

---

[223] Ibid.

simultaneous use of the intellect;"²²⁴ this idea proposes proportionality and restrain; it also allows the incorporation of a concept of (gradual) escalation which can serve the political purpose of the war. The reason for this is that the proportional use of force avoids pushing the adversary to extremes by useless slaughter, which can also be used to influence moral force. Maximal force without restrain will give advantage in the short term, but fail in the long run. Clausewitz makes a distinction between wars between states and savage war. In the case of war between states, the absolutist variety, is a "far less cruel and destructive than war between savage."²²⁵

For Clausewitz, the reasons lie in the degree of civilization of the society waging the war and in its underlying motives being "hostile feeling and[/or] hostile intentions."²²⁶ Hostile intentions are normally attributes of *inter-state* war and are seen as more rational, while hostile feeling, which appeals to passions, are more attributes of what Clausewitz calls *savage* war. If the first type tends to rein in violence, the second propagates it. If hostile feeling are not contained and they develop into a "passionate hatred for each other,"²²⁷ war may tend toward its extreme form. In the present, one can suggest that such extreme forms can be seen in the treatment of subdued populations or prisoners of ISIS, for example. However, in the history of COIN, a prime example may be the result of the repression of the War in Vendée in 1796 and the resulting massacre.

To render the enemy powerless, the aim is to disarm him. To do so, the enemy must be put "in a situation that is even more unpleasant than the sacrifice you call on him to make,"²²⁸ and this situation should last long enough for the adversary to admit his defeat. The more recent problems, which Clausewitz would not have confronted, are the nihilist tendency of some adversaries at a tactical level and the blood feud concept of others, which may have an influence at operational or strategic levels.

---

224 Clausewitz, *On War*, 75.
225 Ibid., 76.
226 Ibid.
227 Ibid.
228 Ibid., 77.

In the last decade, a majority of the adversaries have sought to die for their cause, because in their view the outcome is better than life. This development poses a fundamental question: what situation is more unpleasant than death? In this case, the answer may be to be defenseless and a prisoner, or at least contained, as life would be more "unpleasant" than death. The knowledge of the enemy does not reside only in numbers of weapons systems or physical strength, but also in his moral force.

Jeffrey B. Cozzens, in his article, "Victory: From the Prism of Jihadi Culture,"[229] does an interesting analysis of such a situation and concludes that the metrics used with a Western approach cannot function in such a case. The protracted conflicts of the last decades are partially a result of the omission that "war ... is not the action of a living force upon a lifeless mass"[230] but as Fred Kaplan reminds us with a quote from Clausewitz, that the "enemy has a vote"[231] and the ally too.[232] The analysis of an adversary must be done within the adversary's own cultural sphere, as Colonel John Boyd explained in his theory of the Observe-Orient-Decide-Act (OODA) loops, not in another foreign and or abstract template. This idea was also expressed by Clausewitz: "you must match your effort against his power of resistance ... *the total means at his disposal* and the *strength of his will.*"[233] The means are the resort of intelligence gathering; however. the strength of will is not defined by a single number in an order of battle.

As explained previously, there is a cause-and-effect relationship as the enemy will is influenced by one's will. However, Western states shall not forget that history may play a bigger role in the adversary's will to resist than what was previously thought, as it has happened far too often: "This is not an opinion held by one or two people. I never met an Afghan who did not hold the view that the British were in Helmand to screw them. They hated the British viscerally and histori-

---

[229] Jeffrey B. Cozzens, "Victory from the Prism of Jihadi Culture," *Joint Force Quarterly*, no. 52 (January 2009).
[230] Clausewitz, *On War*, 77.
[231] Kaplan, *Insurgents*, 51.
[232] Clausewitz, *On War*, 79.
[233] Ibid., 77.

cally,"[234] and then Ledwidge lamented that the "unfortunate fact was the British had forgotten their history."[235]

War is neither sudden nor spontaneous, and causes are to be discovered in past events;[236] the problem is they do not always seem obvious to the one who searches them, especially when this search is hampered by ignorance or cultural bias. As remarked by Clausewitz, the opponent is not an "abstract person to the other."[237] Osama bin Laden, the Taliban, or the Iraqi army and people were long known to political and military figures in the West, at least since the late 1970s. Having originated in Arab nationalism, fomented, in turn, by Nazi policy to the Arab world against Great Britain, as well as the U.S. strategy in the Arab world against the USSR, Osama bin Laden made his "Declaration of Jihad on the Americans Occupying the Country of the Two Sacred Places"[238] in 1996, five years before the tragic events of September 11, 2001. The Taliban were supported by the United States against the Soviets following the invasion of Afghanistan by the USSR in 1979. Finally, Iraq was not a new problem and was well studied in the 1980s, already a scene of war in the 1980s and in the famous case of 1990–1991, however, in this particular case with other ends and goals, limited in scope. Modern Iraq arose in the collapse of the Ottoman Empire and with the French and British conquest of this territory in 1914–1918 and their attempt to rule it in the interim.

There is a tendency in Western civilization, because of wrongheaded military professionalism and civilian naïveté, to see war as a short and contained event; after all, World War I "should" have been over by December 1914 As Clausewitz would point out, however, war is not resolved in "a single short blow"[239] and war is not finished

---

[234] Ledwidge, *Losing Small Wars,* 104.

[235] Ibid., 64.

[236] Clausewitz, *On War,* 78.

[237] Ibid.

[238] National Commission on Terrorist Attacks upon the United States, *The Foundation of the New Terrorism* (accessed on May 15, 2015), http://www.9-11commission.gov/report/911Report_Ch2.htm.

[239] Clausewitz, *On War,* 79.

before peace is signed by all parties. If signing a peace treaty with a state is easy to do at the end of hostilities, no one can say the same with insurgencies. Insurgencies, if they fail, tend to continue with meaningless fighting with terrorism tactics, before vanishing without a peace treaty. The trick is to determine whether hostilities are really ended or just postponed, and can lead to a longer mobilization of forces than necessary; as Clausewitz argues, "in war the result is never final."[240]

For a state to assure the best outcome, the theater must be stabilized long enough to ensure favorable conditions for a long and lasting peace. In some cases, the full might of a state cannot be applied in a single blow. As mentioned before, there are phases in war. The coalition did well until Phase IV. This is when politics coincides again with military operations, although because of the constant dialogue between the levels, a longer commitment should not be a surprise.

For Clausewitz, "War is merely the continuation of [government][241] policy by [or with] other means;"[242] meanwhile, Antulio J. Echevarria II, in *Clausewitz and Contemporary War*, equates "politik" to "international relations."[243] With Clausewitz's definition, a case can be made for small wars; however, with Echevarria's addendum, war can only be an inter-state war, which is plainly not the case in the record of war now and then. War starts and ends due to a state's policy toward a situation. The higher the importance of this policy for the state, the less a state will disengage from it. This is also true for the adversary. This explains why WWI and WWII reached the most extreme forms of warfare known at that time before the atomic era; vital national interests of multiple countries were at stake. Such situations also called for the unconditional surrender of a side to allow the other to survive. In recent conflicts, such vital interests for a state have not been present on both sides. This resulted in the Alliance by a

---

[240] Ibid., 80.

[241] Peter Paret, *Clausewitz and the State: the Man, His Histories, and His Times* (Princeton, NJ: Princeton University Press, 2007), 387.

[242] Clausewitz, *On War*, 87.

[243] Antulio J. Echevarria, II, *Clausewitz and Contemporary War* (New York: Oxford University Press, 2007), 4.

lesser mobilization of states' capacities and willingness to fight to the end; thus, for the alliance, the "policy is directed only toward minor objective, the emotions of the masses will be little stirred and they will have to be stimulated rather than held back,"[244] a thought echoed by Andrew Bacewich's in *Breach of Trust*.

The same cannot be said for the insurgencies in Iraq or Afghanistan: their "national vital interests" where at stake, especially their political survival. Subsequently, political aims and military aims did not always converge, and due to a mismanagement of strategy, they were not sufficiently reconciled. In other words, the means used did not match the needs of the policy.

War is also a question of polarization, according to the dialectic that is core to Clausewitz's theoretical method to realize his ideas. For Clausewitz, this polarization refers to a single object. Only one side can win a specific battle; therefore, the other loses the battle. This fact is handy as long as both sides use the same measures of profit and loss for the same event. However, as demonstrated by Jeffrey B. Cozzens with Iraq and Afghanistan, the Alliance and its nemesis neither referred to the same event nor used the same referential. This reality led to divergent narratives. With the help of connectivity in today's world, the core audiences were led to divergent conclusions. Such a situation produced a protracted conflict, because both sides were "winning" from their own perspectives or ways of measuring victory.

The rapid operational and tactical successes of the Alliance first in Afghanistan in late 2001 and then in Iraq for a brief time in 2003 were not a real surprise. Shock and Awe functioned at the lower levels of war, against a symmetrical adversary, as its proponents would no doubt readily propose. But soon enough, the asymmetry in the ends and means for the combat changed as these conflicts became protracted and attritional as they naturally must do in nearly all cases. Clausewitz explains two factors which produce a suspension in military actions: "the superiority of [the] defense over [the] attack" and "the imperfect knowledge of the situation."[245]

---

[244] Clausewitz, *On War*, 88.

[245] Clausewitz, *On War*, 84.

As the Alliance's nemeses were pushed back into a defensive position, they had, in Clausewitz's view, the advantage of the defense over the attack. The factor time is working for the "defenders." As the Afghan proverb said, "You have the watches; we have the time."[246] This fact was equally true in Iraq. Insurgencies benefit from the time factor when levied against the factors of anger and hatred in democratic nations, especially where an expeditionary army on a small scale wages such a war. Faulty intelligence, or faulty interpretation of it, in both theaters of wars, led to grave misunderstandings from reality; Ledwidge explained from his personal experience how bad assessments led to wrong actions and concluded "that was the reality. The *virtual* reality, in which the military HQ lived, was that this was a well-run cordon-and-search operation."[247] The intelligence community does not particularly appreciate Clausewitz for his views on intelligence,[248] but the Iraq case with the weapons of mass destruction controversy[249] proved that, notwithstanding all new means to collect intelligence that one can possess since Napoleon's time, the result may still sometimes be blurry.

So far, the nature of war, as Clausewitz described it, has nonetheless not changed in the way that van Creveld and his acolytes in the present would have it. Technology has improved forces and changed tactical fighting, but this change does not affect the underlying truth of war, the friction and the risk and chance native to war. General Daniel Bolger recognizes in *Why We Lost* that

> though training, good leadership, mission rehearsal, and certain equipment ... help accommodate friction. Certain modern information technology proponents even claim to be able to end friction altogether through near-perfect situational awareness. No hardware or software, though, removes the tired, confused, scared human from the equation.[250]

---

[246] Ledwidge, *Losing Small Wars*, 88.
[247] Ibid., 81. Emphasis in the original.
[248] Clausewitz, *On War*, 84, 117–118.
[249] William Rivers Pitt and Scott Ritter, *War on Iraq: What Team Bush Doesn't Want You to Know* (New York: Context Books, 2002).
[250] Bolger, *Why We Lost*, 28.

Friction and chance is also evoked by Machiavelli in *The Prince*: "Fortune governs one half of our actions, but even so she leaves the half more or less in our power to control."[251] In order to control the second half, genius and courage are needed. The genius and the courage needed by the ones who participate in those wars still remain a part of it, as described by Clausewitz and still recognized by Gentile: "War at its most basic level is about death and destruction. Counterinsurgency warfare is no different, and its result on the ground can be as destructive as conventional warfare."[252] This is a truth that a new generation has learned at great pain, while the political class in the United States, at least in some quarters, partakes of this pain and suffering as a political weapon in domestic strife far from the war itself.

The knowledge as well as intelligence remains principal factors to assess in which contest one is prepared to enter and ultimately, the factors mass and time, still makes a difference whatever technological edge one's possess. On intelligence, Freeman remarks rightly that "with improved information gathering, Clausewitz's advice to ignore timely intelligence now appears as more of a recipe for disaster than a mean of avoiding unnecessary panic."[253] Technology insofar may not have totally dispersed the "fog of war," for a part of it lies in the past events and the interpretation done of them. The second part lies in the policies, and not only in the battlefield, but the reading through the "fog of war" has improved since Clausewitz's reticence toward intelligence.

Adversaries still have a voice in the ballot and use it, today even more so, thanks to global connectivity. Finally, war remains a matter of policy, which linked hatred, chances, and reasons has before, at least since Thucydides named the "three very powerful motives… security, honor, and self-interest"[254] that led to war. So far, nihilism is the only factor not accounted for by Clausewitz that has been presented by some of today's adversaries.

---

[251] Cited in Freedman, *Strategy*, 51.
[252] Gentile, *Wrong Turn*, 7.
[253] Freedman, *Strategy*, 89.
[254] Thucydides, Rex Warner, and M. I. Finley, *History of the Peloponnesian War*, (New York, NY: Penguin Books, 1972), 80.

B. CLAUSEWITZ'S TRINITY IN ACTUAL WAR WITH NON-STATE ACTORS

Some will argue that Clausewitz's interpretations cannot be used in guerilla warfare with non-state actors, since one cannot distinguish, in this case, between a state, an army, and a people. Such an interpretation fails to grasp what Clausewitz intends, with the idea of actual war as being made up of (a) political purpose, (b) chance, and (c) the passions of anger and hatred within psychology and politics. These elements constitute war in reality versus war in theory and help one to understand the two kinds of war in reality. This author argues that Clausewitz can be applied to a regional warlord as well as to a state with the caveat that the higher level of government must be weak enough and not to be able to enforce its own rules. Part of the key is given by Clausewitz in *On War*, Book Eight, Chapter Four.

There is something basic to keep in mind here. First, terrorism is a tactic of fighting, nothing else; it is neither a form of government of any strength, nor is it a grand strategy worthy of the name.[255] Second, terrorists are actors who seek a political and ideological goal; if terrorist equals insurgent, their goal is to control a territory for their own sake. That means the insurgents research the attributes of a state to impose new borders in which they can rule with their own form of government and policies by the use of their own power, which, if recognized, becomes legitimate.

In *The Transformation of Warfare*, van Creveld's view on war seems to be inaccurate and as such merely embodies an old misreading of Clausewitz, especially in the British school of strategy since 1914. We may reject some part of Clausewitz, but the trinity is a way of understanding war in fact versus in theory, and the distinction between total war and limited war is central to all who want to wage a war. Clausewitz defined his trinity as follows:

A paradoxical trinity—composed of primordial violence, hatred, and enmity, which are to be regarded as a blind natural force; the play of chance and probabilities within which the creative spirit is free to

---

[255] Chairman of the Joint Chiefs of Staff, *Counterterrorism* (Joint Publication 3–26) (Washington, DC: Department of Defense, October 24, 2014), 18 (I-5).

roam; and its element of subordination, as an instrument of policy, which make it subject to reason alone.[256]

The interpretation of this definition, however, may differ. Until the fall of the Soviet Union in late 1991, both sides, the West and the USSR, had a similar trinity, with the same interpretation. Army = army, state = state politics, and people = people (Table 1). With the Balkan wars, this trinity started to change for some actors as follows: army = warriors, state = political cause of one group, and people = a fraction of the population who supports a group's causes.

Table 1: Trinity Interpretation

	Until 1992		After 1992	
Trinity	**State A**	**State B**	**State A**	**Organization B**
State (Ends) *Will/Reasons*	State	State	State	Political cause of group B
People (Means) *Anger*	People	People	People	Supporter of group B
Army (Ways) *Chances/ Passion*	Army	Army	Army	Warriors of group B
	Symmetrical		*Asymmetrical*	

Adapted from Carl von Clausewitz, *On War*, ed. and trans. Michael Howard and Peter Paret (Princeton, NJ: Princeton University Press, 1984); 89.

Therefore, in order to be capable of operating if the goal is to achieve a lasting result, any group, from a terrorist cell to a state, is based on a trinity. The "state" is the expression for what the war is fought, or the goal—usually a political statement (way of life, right to religion x, right to exist, right to justice, etc.). The people, as in "We the people," are the economic basis to sustain the fight (war effort) and the provider of forces. Any group or organization needs them as

---

[256] Clausewitz, *On War*, 89.

supporters to feed the "green machine," the army, with fresh forces. A state will call them *soldiers*; a non-state group may call them *warriors*. Whatever the name, the function given to them is still to fight for the political aim. Therefore, in this view, every element of fighting is then Clausewitzian in essence and based on a trinity.

However, we may talk about an asymmetry when we put a state in relationship with a group. This asymmetry is not a new phenomenon—think about David and Goliath. At a tactical level, even a symmetrical adversary researches asymmetry in order to limit casualties, which leads Conrad Crane, as a partisan of COIN and a well-educated officer, to say, "There are two types of warfare: asymmetric and stupid."[257] By 1992, the use of asymmetric tactics had simply become more commonly reported in the organized violence that eventuated in that decade in Africa and Southern Europe as the Cold War vanished, and asymmetric tactics have been central to a group's survival as long as the group does not have the same means as the state it is fighting.

The asymmetry is related to the ways, means, and ends that the non-state group employs in a fight. Because of this asymmetry, at the beginning, the group using such strategy and tactics will not match the ones of the state, and may never achieve them. In this case a state is simply analogous to a police operation fighting a sort of *terrorism* (e.g., IRA, Rote Armee Fraktion, ETA, etc.). If the group rises and gains support, the state will then face a *guerrilla or insurgency* (e.g., Vietminh, Hezbollah, ISIS, etc.). Now if the group is effective, the state will face an *army* (e.g., Ushtria Çlirimtare e Kosovës (UCK) the North Vietnamese Army (NVA), etc.).

As the group's means grow over time, and come closer to the group's ends, the groups tends to adapt its ways in a similar way to that of the state. For a group to defeat a state, during this fight, the group's attribute had to become equal to the state's attribute. If effective, the group will finally obtain its will against the state it is fighting (e.g., NVA in Vietnam, UCK in Kosovo). In both of the aforementioned cases, the groups could not have survived if other states had not come to their support. In other words, a new state can emerge

---

[257] Conrad Crane, as cited in Simpson, *War from the Ground Up*, 140.

only if other states authorize it (Vietnam, Kosovo, and South Soudan).

We may extend the comparison to the era prior to the Westphalian states and follow it through until today and find similarities to the prior example of development of ways, means, and ends, but it seems that a comparison of the trinities involved in the conflicts and their respective ends, means, and ways is an effective way to do it. Hence, communal leaders, warlords, or presidents have to build their power on a "trinity" of "chance," "hatred," and "reasons." Referring back to Table 1, such a trinity may also be called "government," "people," and "army;" or "political cause of the group B," "supporter of the group B," and "warriors of the group B." The same parameters of the trinity, such as economic, reliability, and popularity, also apply to any group fighting any state. If a country breaks down after an inter-state–type war and goes into a sectarian-type civil war, the main difference for armed forces is, instead of having to treat one single "trinity," they may have to engage one or more of them according to the number of tribes or warlords in the theater.

The "inter-state paradigm" (0) remains relevant if one does the exercise of mentally subdividing the trinity: for example, giving Taliban A a territory A, against which Coalition C fights, and in that period of time, Taliban B in the province B may or may not be neutral, ally, or enemy, and so on. Clausewitz principles apply independently for a physical state or, an "imagined state." (For example, ISIS, Taliban in Province X in Afghanistan, hackers , etc. However, the "physical" state shall be defined.)

War is a duel between two actors. These actors can be states, groups, or a mix of both. However, both of these actors possess a trinity, which may be influenced by the other; this is the reciprocity of war, according to Clausewitz.

Figure 7, Relationship Between Two Trinities

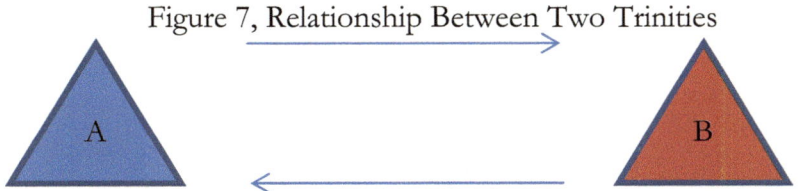

The terrorists or militias may not act with a single rationale[258] because they are not a cohesive unit; militarily speaking, they were similar to a coalition with caveats for each actor. One may still speak about a "single war"[259] as long as the various elements display the same political purpose. In this case, "if you can vanquish all your enemies by defeating one of them, that defeat must be the main objective in the war."[260] As seen in Figure 8, the political fragmentation, such as the one in Afghanistan or Iraq, is not a problem if Coalition A accepts the reality of the Group B fragmentation; thus, they shouldn't be treated as a single adversary but as multiple and different adversaries. In this case, Coalition A has "to act as if there were two wars or even more, each with its own object."[261] In such a situation, Clausewitz argued for caution because the presence of multiple enemies gives them (Group B, in this case) a "consequently great[er] superiority."[262]

Figure 8, Break-down of Trinities

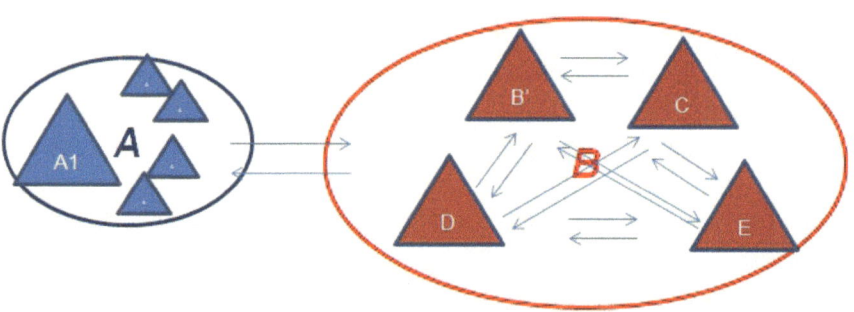

The trick is to adapt "A" trinity against the other trinities to achieve A's goals. As a coalition, it can be difficult to have a chance of

---

[258] Simpson, *War from the Ground Up*, 102.
[259] Clausewitz, *On War*, 596.
[260] Ibid., 596–97.
[261] Ibid., 597.
[262] Ibid.

success unless the coalition assigns one different member to each trinity with overall coordination across DIME (see Figure 9). However, the OODA loops from each actor have to be understood in detail and acted upon in a synchronized manner by A in order to be successful.

Figure 9, Assignment of Trinities within a Coalition

Van Creveld, in his preemptive dismissal of Clausewitz's trinity, halted the debate on its usefulness. In fact, nothing speaks against a plurality of trinities colliding and shifting alliances. Clausewitz may refer to a "bilateral polarity" because he defines war as a duel between two nation-states, hence two trinities. Two alliances such as the ones of the Cold War, are pretty rare in the global history of warfare. One adversary may be engaged at a time, but the second one may be on his way. This is when maneuver starts to be relevant to divide them, make separate peace, and conquer the rest, one at the time. The problem is such a way to work cannot support Manichean politics, neither global nor bold statements. It has to be tailored case after case, and it may be discussed multiple times; this marks a breaking point between military "strategy" and political strategy (or strategy.) Military "strategy" gives three options: winning, stalemate, or losing. But the political strategy defines them and gives playing room to coerce enemies into dialogue, especially if the political strategy allows room for dialogue instead of unconditional surrender or death: "War is only a branch of political activity; that it is in no sense autonomous."[263]

---

[263] Clausewitz, *On War*, 605.

C. THE MISUSE AND MISINTERPRETATION OF "STRATEGY"

Historians and scholars are fortunate, because they are able to analyze facts with enough time elapsed to allow them to form theories or a story line about a given event. After all, this task is exactly what Clausewitz proposed with his idea of critical thought being made up of the three parts: (a) chronology, (b) cause and effect, and (c) judgment.[264] In the atmosphere after 9/11, decisions had to be made and action had to be taken by senior U.S. leaders as much for domestic political reasons as out of shock at the apparent violence of an attack on the continental United States. However, fourteen years after the event, the first conclusion is that the Alliance failed to think about Clausewitz's first strategic question in *On War*:

The first, the supreme, the most far-reaching act of judgment that the statesman and commander have to make is to establish by that test the kind of war on which they are embarking; neither mistaking it for, nor trying to turn it into, something that is alien to its nature.[265]

This statement implies first a dialogue between the statesman and the commander, as well as commanders who are versed in the varieties of war and in the appropriate military response at the three levels of war. Michael R. Gordon in *COBRA II: The Inside Story of the Invasion and Occupation of Iraq* explains how such dialogue almost never happened surrounding the invasion of Iraq in 2003, and Kaplan confirms that strategy was missing in both cases beyond toppling Saddam Hussein and the assault on the Taliban.[266] Second, Clausewitz implies that the assessment is done at all levels without forgetting the local and global role of history. Ledwidge shows how the history of British troops in Afghanistan in the nineteenth century was forgotten or ignored, as well as in Iraq, and he also points out that, despite all evidence at hand in its rich variety, Western states did not learn the lessons from the Soviet engagement in Afghanistan during the 1980s. However, today's problem regarding strategy and history is addressed by Douglas Porch in *Counterinsurgency: Exposing the Myths of the New*

---

[264] Ibid., 156.

[265] Ibid., 88.

[266] Kaplan, *Insurgents*, 363.

Way of War, who remarks, based on Francis Fukuyama's work, "History has lost the value to inform strategy, because ideology, technology, and doctrine now substitute for strategy."[267] The third implication of Clausewitz's statement is that this assessment must be realistic in content, means, ways, end, and time; and fourth, that the main goal shall not be alien to the means; nation-building is not a military capacity.

Hew Strachan assesses the discrepancy between strategy, policy, and operational level and argues that a misreading of Clausewitz and a misunderstanding of the period in which *On War* was written has led to today's misconceptions and mixing of concepts. "Strategy has been shaped above all by considerations of space and time;"[268] strategy is about applying means to ends in a particular case. Thus, "strategy lies at the interface between operational capabilities and political objectives" and it is "based on the recognition of the nature of war itself." However, there are caveats; strategy should be thought "within a particular theater of war"[269] and "should serve the ends of policy."[270] Strategy is also a dialogue with policy: "Strategy is designed to make war useable by the state, so that he can, if need be, use forces to fulfil its political objectives. … it exists in relation with policy, politic, and diplomacy."[271]

---

[267] Douglas Porch, *Counterinsurgency: Exposing the Myths of the New Way of War* (New York: Cambridge University Press, 2013), 333.
[268] Strachan, *Direction of War*, 11.
[269] Strachan, *Direction of War*, 15.
[270] Ibid., 12.
[271] Ibid., 43.

Figure 10, Interactivity of Strategy and Policy into the Realm of Diplomacy and Politic

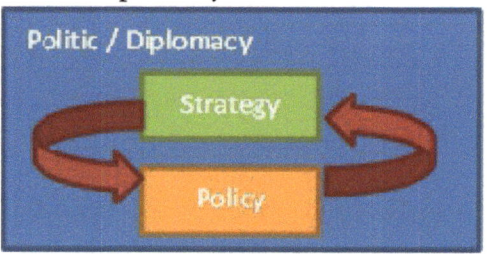

"Strategy" is almost certainly the most misused word today; in many books and scholarly articles, strategy comes as a direct translation of either Jomini or Clausewitz, without being adapted to today's military vocabulary. Clausewitz's and Jomini's interpretations of strategy were closer to today's meaning for "operational art."

With centuries passing, societal and industrial changes, and technological evolution, military vocabulary has adapted and become richer in terminology. Until the late 1800s, military planners referred only to tactics and strategy. By the beginning of the 1900s, in the vein of Helmut von Moltke, military planners introduced operational art. Operational art retained a certain amount of the substance of the prior term, strategy, but not all. Until the beginning of the 20th century, strategy was mainly the art of moving self-sufficient armies from a staging sector to a battlefield. With the industrialization of war, although armies were doing the fighting, the logistic of sustaining armies decided the contest. The needed reorganization of the society after the mobilization to keep the "wheels turning" became a bigger challenge than drafting soldiers for the front. The state had to look to the bigger picture in order to keep the supply flowing to the front. Thus, to support operations, the state had to coordinate its industrial might with its society, thus having an impact on its internal, external, and diplomatic politics. The art of winning war, "military strategy," became a subset of national strategy, focused on aligning the means of the state to the ways of the army, to achieve the goals of the policies. So the strategy of today is not Clausewitz's strategy anymore.[272]

Clausewitz teaches: "Tactics teaches the use of armed forces in the engagement; strategy, the use of engagements for the object of the war."[273] The object of the war is a political goal.[274] Clausewitz continues: "Strategy ... assigns a particular aim to it [engagements];"[275] thus, "policy, then, will permeate all military operations, and in so far as their violent nature will admit, it will have a continuous influence on them."[276] Today, although influenced by the policy of the state, this statement is close to the definition of the operational level of war.

But Clausewitz sensed that strategy was also more: "Dealing as it does with ends which bear directly on the restoration of peace. ... As these ends will have to be considered primarily by the commander-in-chief."[277] If Clausewitz admits that strategy can be done in the homeland capital instead as in the theater of war, he also warns that both have to be geographically close.[278] In his time, the commander-in-chief was often the political leader of the country, bearing both tasks. When a political leader merges with a military leader, the state is closer to a dictatorship than a democracy; thus, this template is no longer valid in democracy without adaptations. However, "Only in the highest realms of strategy that intellectual complications and extreme diversity of factors and relationships occur. At that level there is little or no difference between strategy, policy and statesman-

---

[272] Nor should Clausewitz's definition of strategy be confounded with Corbett's "Major Strategy," which equals the sum of the forces, politics, diplomacy, and the economic which is a function of commerce and financial capacities of a state (Strachan, *Direction of War*, 15). Neither with Fuller's view that "Peace Strategy" should be equated with "War Strategy" (Strachan, *Direction of War*, 16) as the first one has to prepare the second one before the conflict arise.
[273] Clausewitz, *On War*, 128.
[274] Ibid., 87.
[275] Ibid., 143.
[276] Ibid., 87.
[277] Ibid., 147.
[278] Clausewitz, *On War*, 177.

ship."[279] When continuing and exposing the "elements of strategy,"[280] Clausewitz makes it clear that his definition of strategy is today's "operational art" and not today's "(national) strategy."

For Jomini, *strategy* is not only one of the "five principal parts" of "the art of war,"[281] but it also encompasses thirteen points. The first two, "selection of the theater of war" and the "determination of the decisive points"[282] may be close to today's strategy. Unlike Clausewitz, Jomini by his definition, willingly sets aside political and moral interactions; for him, this is part of the *Military Policy*[283] (political guidance for the army) and the *Diplomatic Art*,[284] and he wished to concentrate only on the military aspects in his *Art of War*.

Both Clausewitz and Jomini recognized the higher implications of such state's instruments, as politics and diplomacy, economy and industry, people and moral. If Clausewitz linked the state's instruments with war through his trinity, Jomini willingly put it aside; however, both concentrated mainly on what is today the operational level of war. Thus, both books, *On War* and *The Art of War*, have to be read today by translating *strategy* into *operational art*.

Today, strategy is the "art" of coordinating the national policy with the diplomatic, military, informational, and economic spheres to mutually support each other. This is also the art of "tailoring" the interaction of these spheres to respond to a specific problem.[285] A strategy is unique and serves only one conflict. Moreover, strategy is not a static element; strategy is a "two way bridge"[286] and needs a permanent dialogue between the head of the state and the leading military

---

[279] Ibid., 178.

[280] Clausewitz, *On War*, 183.

[281] Antoine Henri Jomini, *The Art of War*, 66.

[282] Jomini, *The Art of War*, trans. Charles Messenger (London: Greenhill Books, 1992), 68–69.

[283] Ibid., 15–16. *Military policy* "is the name given to them; for they belong exclusively neither to diplomacy nor to strategy, but are still of the highest importance in the plans both of a statesman and a general."

[284] Ibid., 38

[285] Simpson, *War from the Ground Up*, 135.

[286] Ibid., 233.

general (commander-in-chief). Strategy has to be coordinated to efficiently support the DIME spheres and facilitate their intercourse to achieve the main end state "with ends which bear directly on the restoration of peace."[287] This led Strachan to postulate: "Strategy therefore has to rest on an understanding of war and war's nature because it will shape policy."[288]

Policies should be linked to regional realities or military capabilities.[289] However, "war is distinct from policy,"[290] but "once they are engaged in a conflict those policies are shaped by the action of the adversary," as the enemy also has a vote, and "that interaction itself creates an independent dynamic, which is both incremental and unpredictable."[291] Thus, "policy provides the logic of war"[292] and should answer such questions as "where were these wars to be fought, against whom, and for what purpose?"[293]

Peace is a political act, not a military one; this also reinforces the role of the statesman on one side and the military leader on the other. Each has to work in his sphere, but the political sphere encompasses the military one; however, if the political leader gives the bearing of the strategy at a national level, the military leader stirs the operational level to reach the bearings. Strachan summarizes it well: "Assessing the character of an individual war seems to be a task for the military professional—is it regular or irregular, high intensity or low intensity? But the answer has profound political implications."[294] This requires a constant dialogue and adaptation of plans between top military leaders and the political level—the two-way bridge. In other words, the micromanagement from Rumsfeld in the military conduct of the Afghanistan and the Iraq conflicts was more detrimental to the out-

---

[287] Clausewitz, *On War*, 147.
[288] Strachan, *Direction of War*, 14.
[289] Ibid., 11.
[290] Ibid., 13.
[291] Strachan, *Direction of War*, 13.
[292] Ibid., 28.
[293] Ibid., 67.
[294] Strachan, *Direction of War*, 62–63.

come, because it impeached the coordination of the military-political level and it impaired on the leeway that the military leadership must give in their own spheres of competence to be efficient.

This fact is also not new. This is the Jominian approach versus the Clausewitzian approach of military control. However, at the end, both concede the same point. The political aim of war is given by the government. "Military strategy" has to be decided between both levels, political and military. But once the operation starts, the military conducts it, not the government. Sometimes during ongoing operations, situations change: "Professional judgment may run counter to political priorities, and that these clashes need to be confronted and debated, not denied."[295]

When Rumsfeld said once, "You do the fighting, I'll do the talking,"[296] he was right: the political level communicates. However, it does not need to interfere in the fighting options. If needed, this interference should be done by a change of policy or strategic goal. To conduct operations, the government influences the military by changing the content of the political goal they are aiming for. This also requires that military leaders are apolitical in their jobs (not seeking personal interest through political intrigues).

Using "strategy" at all levels only brings confusion, and the best example may be the "counterinsurgency strategy"; it may have been a "military strategy" in Clausewitzian or Jominian terms, or an operational approach in today's vocabulary, but certainly not a national strategy, as Sir Hew Strachan points out in *The Direction of War: Contemporary Strategy in Historical Perspective*,[297] and Emile Simpson in *War from the Ground Up: Twenty-First Century Combat as Politics*:

Counter-insurgency in Afghanistan [or Iraq] is frequently described as a strategy. It isn't. Counter-insurgency is an operational approach: a method which organises actions in service of a strategy, but not a strategy in itself ... it can erroneously suggest that counter-insurgency

---

[295] Ibid, 74.
[296] Ibid., 75.
[297] Strachan, *Direction of War*, 117–18.

doctrine can be applied regardless of political context as a strategy in itself, as opposed to being the operational component of a strategy.[298]

The second part of the problem with strategy and the political interaction with the military sphere is twofold: first, even if Jomini recognizes the political and diplomatic dimension, he did not analyze their implications in depth in *The Art of War*; hence, he provides little advice to generals on how to handle the translation of the political will in the military might. Second, Clausewitz did in-depth analyses of the political dimension, and also the diplomatic implication by extension; however, little advice was given on how to coordinate the DIME. In both cases, their analyses were vertical. In the words of Simpson, "Jomini ... writes about warfare rather than war. Clausewitz on the other contrary writes to explain war, shaped by society and politics, as it functions according to means and ends."[299]

The results of the Afghanistan and Iraq conflicts show this dichotomy. According to Gentile, "In Afghanistan, good strategy has been absent from the start";[300] and Kaplan asserted for Iraq that the main finding of the Wolfowitz team in Iraq in January 2004 was "that American forces had *no* [Kaplan's emphasis] overall strategy."[301] General George Casey, in May 2004, complained along the same lines, as did Condoleezza Rice in May 2006, three years into the conflict. This is also what the future president would hear from Admiral Mike Mullen concerning Afghanistan in November 2008 during the transition, seven years into the conflict.[302] In both cases, as long as it was only a military matter at the operational level, allied forces were successful until the end of Phase III. Jomini is, after all, the most studied military thinker in U.S. military circles, and "Phase IV worries America."[303] Stuart Kinross *in Clausewitz in America* remarks that "the lack of a clear policy for countering insurgency in Iraq suggest that

---

[298] Simpson, *War from the Ground Up*, 131.
[299] Ibid., 136.
[300] Gentile, *Wrong Turn*, 118.
[301] Kaplan, *Insurgents*, 83
[302] Kaplan, *Insurgents*, 83, 96, 194–95, 295.
[303] Gordon and Trainor, *Cobra II,* 106.

the U.S. may have returned full circle to the flawed strategic approach evident in Vietnam."[304]

As soon as the political and diplomatic level had to merge on the theater of war, there was no more strategy at national level, as Kaplan in *The Insurgents* and Gordon in *Cobra II* analyze in their books.[305] Clausewitz, although he was widely studied in the aftermath of the Vietnam War, lost influence after the Gulf War of 1990–1991 and its success on the strategic and operational levels. As Gordon remarked, "The public debate over COIN's utility in contemporary conflict suffers from confusion as to whether COIN is an operational approach, a strategy or a policy."[306] Consequently, everybody was talking about "strategy," but meaning "operational level," and did not coordinate with the political-decision-making level in a coherent way.

This situation also eventually led to a misevaluation of the kind of war in which troops were sent into. The war that started had changed by the end of the opening campaigns. The meaning of this change was not seized upon by those responsible for the formation of strategy and for its political legitimacy under the constitution. As Freedman reminds us, strategy is to "take a view of the system as a whole and assess the position of the individual parts."[307]

D. PURPOSE AND MEANS OF WAR

For Clausewitz, three broad objectives can summarize the activities of war: destroying the fighting capacities of the adversary, occupying the country to impair the enemy's capacities to rebuild, and breaking the enemy's will so the war can end.[308] However, the corollary can be that although a territory may be occupied, resistance can occur inside, with or without the help of an ally. In Clausewitz words "not every war necessarily leads to a final decision and settlement."[309]

---

[304] Kinross, *Clausewitz and America*, 190.
[305] Kaplan, *Insurgents*; Binden, as cited in Gordon and Trainor, *Cobra II*, 106.
[306] Simpson, *War from the Ground Up*, 145.
[307] Freedman, *Strategy*, 478.
[308] Clausewitz, *On War*, 90.
[309] Ibid.

In Iraq, the fighting forces (Iraqi army) were destroyed and brought under submission. The country was occupied. However, the will of the resistance was not totally broken. Clausewitz continues, "But the aim of disarming the enemy is in fact not always encountered in reality and need not be fully achieved as a condition of peace."[310] Even if Clausewitz does not take the enemy's disarmament as a law, it may be preferable in some cases because it can shorten the engagement. In the Iraq case, the aim was a regime change, not to retain Iraq as a prize. This was a political alternative to a military campaign. By removing Saddam Hussein, the will of the adversary was destroyed, and Iraq could be occupied.

Occupation is a risky business today as it has been in the past: "We may occupy a country completely, but hostilities can be renewed again in the interior, or perhaps with allied help."[311] The adversary was not the Iraqi army per se, but Saddam Hussein; thus, the disbandment of the Iraqi army by Presidential Envoy Paul Bremer with the "Coalition Provisional Authority Order Number 2"[312] created a new adversary with a new will of resistance, despite the fact that the alliance needed the Iraqi Army to secure the country. Bremer ignored the idea that "disarming the enemy … is in fact not always encountered in reality, and need not be fully achieved as a condition of peace."[313] As the country was occupied and even more insecure than before, it gave the precondition needed for insurgency to arise.

Unlike the insurgencies in China and Vietnam, which operated as one unit, Iraq and Afghanistan, due to their societal model, produced multiple insurgencies, all with different agendas. But the mechanism that brought them into existence is the same as for the October Revolution of 1917 or Mao's seizure of power. First, they all profited from a vacuum of power (absence of the Tsar armies, withdrawal from the

---

[310] Ibid., 91.

[311] Ibid., 90.

[312] Paul L. Bremer, "Coalition Provisional Authority Order Number 2" (accessed May 15, 2015), http://www.iraqcoalition.org/regulations/20030823_CPAORD_2_Dissolution_of_Entities_with_Annex_A.pdf.

[313] Clausewitz, *On War*, 91.

Red army out of Manchuria), leading to a vacuum of security; second, they all profited from weapons left by the previous armies. In the Iraqi case, the absence of security at the end of a military operation and the disbandment of the Iraqi army provided the conditions for insurgency to occur. This also occurred in Afghanistan to some extent due to the removal of some warlords and the Taliban, who were providing better security than the Afghan police.[314]

Like in China and Vietnam, the insurgency in Iraq and Afghanistan had the means to develop. Insurgent groups fight for ideology, power, or other intents such as killing the infidel, but at the end of the fight, the gain will be measured in square meters gained over the enemy. The end game for an insurgent in Afghanistan, in Iraq, or even for ISIS is to be able to rule a country physically delimited, a province, a city, or a caliphate. The insurgency phase is a pivot. If things are done properly, the peace is achievable; if not done properly, however, it can be painfully problematic. Clausewitz explains why insurgents benefit from the time factor: the advantage of the defense. This is when the insurgents build up their forces, test their enemy, and learn their trade at fighting to be able to move on the offensive, because if the insurgents want to finally control their territory, they have to move to the offense in a later phase. However, during this period, the enemy acquires an advantage which "need only be enough to *balance* [his emphasis] any superiority the [insurgent's] opponent may possess: in the end his political object will not seem worth the efforts of it cost."[315]

This is exactly what happened in Iraq and Afghanistan. The adversaries of the coalition balanced the advantage of the coalition. And, unwillingly, the coalition helped, because it did not provide security directly after the termination of Phase III. Kilcullen also recognized this problem:

If you fail to create a basic minimum level of security and predictability for ordinary people on the street, it doesn't matter what else you

---

[314] See Ledwidge, *Losing Small Wars*, 71, 81, 83, 209.
[315] Clausewitz, *On War*, 94.

try to do, because none of it is ever likely to happens ... it's impossible ... to get to the underlying issues that need to be addressed.[316]

The absence of security was inexplicable and detrimental. Abraham H. Maslow, the American psychologist, has explained the "hierarchy of needs"[317] in 1943, using the well-known image of a pyramid. The base of this pyramid is the physiological needs of a human being, directly followed by safety, and then upwards until a person can reach self-actualization at the top of the five stages. This alone should be sufficient for any planner to understand the need to provide security to restore a viable society without a vacuum of power between Phase III and Phase IV. Sir Ian Forbes in "Future Warfare and the Principles of War" remarks that in 2005, "The troop-to-population density in Afghanistan is currently 100 times less than Bosnia or Kosovo at the same, post-conflict phase."[318]

This deficiency is explained by the will of the Pentagon political chiefs to have a "leaner" force for fighting. Fighting is a different process than stabilization, which has different needs. A leaner force did the job, and did it well. But directly behind should have been an additional force to take over the safety of the people at the core. In peacetime in Washington, DC, in 2010, the officer-to-citizen ratio was 65.5 to 10,000.[319] The population of Iraq was almost 31 million.[320] At this rate, Iraq would have needed more than 202,000 trained officers patrolling the streets; this number does not count for the "police employee" siting in an office or in a ministry. Globalsecurity.org reports, "As of May 31, 2010, there were approximately 297,000 provincial

---

[316] David Kilcullen, *Out of the Mountains: The Coming Age of the Urban Guerrilla* (New York: Oxford University Press, 2013), 264.

[317] Abraham H. Maslow, "A Theory of Human Motivation," *Psychological Review* 50, 370–96 (1943), http://psychclassics.yorku.ca/Maslow/motivation.htm.

[318] Ian Forbes, "Future Warfare and the Principles of War," in *Rethinking the Principles of War*, ed. Anthony McIvor (Annapolis, MD: Naval Institute Press, 2005), 151.

[319] Governing, "Law Enforcement Officers Per Capita for Cities, Local Departments," table, accessed April 24, 2015, http://www.governing.com/gov-data/safety-justice/law-enforcement-police-department-employee-totals-for-cities.html.

[320] World Bank, Data: Iraq, accessed April 24, 2015, http://data.worldbank.org/country/iraq.

police forces (IPS and Iraqi Civil Defense Directorate)";[321] this figure is assumed to be a total of officers and employees. The question is, why were there so few soldiers patrolling?

If John McGrath was correct when he said, "However, by 2005 noncombat elements had risen proportionally to three fourths of the force size, primarily because of the mass employment of civilian contractors in Iraq in the new millennium,"[322] with the tail-to-tooth ratio of ¾ at the tail and ¼ at the front, the question of Clausewitz's "mass" is certainly central. For the 202,000 officers at the front, the rear would have been a mere 600,000 or a total of almost 800,000 men fielded. Washington, DC, is the U.S. city with the most police officers per capita. But even in Detroit, which has roughly half the number of police officers than Washington, DC, the number of military personal would have been more than what was present at the time in Iraq. The invasion worked out with a lean force, but not the stabilization; General Shinseki and others were right in their estimations prior to the Iraq Invasion, and Rumsfeld was not.[323] As Forbes, echoing Clausewitz,[324] remarks, "a military plan cannot be viewed in isolation and the military cannot be the key actor in an intervention strategy."[325]

By using forces that were too lean, the insurgency was permitted to survive and finally to thrive. Insurgents such as ISIS had the time to learn and export their knowledge to others. Leaner coordinated forces are good for the fight, but not for the stabilization. If the annihilation of the Iraqi army was a matter of technology, this same technology could not replace the "boots on the ground" when the fight went toward a principle of attrition to suffocate an insurgency. According

---

[321] GlobalSecurity.org, "Iraqi Police Service (IPS)," last modified December 1, 2012, http://www.globalsecurity.org/intell/world/iraq/ips.htm.

[322] John J. McGrath, "The Other End of the Spear: The Tooth-to-Tail Ratio (T3R) in Modern Military Operations," in *The Long War Series Occasional Paper 23, Combat Studies* (Fort Leavenworth, KS: Institute Press, 2007), 73.

[323] Bolger, *Why We Lost*, 118–19.

[324] "War should never be thought of as something autonomous but always as an instrument of policy," in von Clausewitz, *On War*, 88.

[325] Forbes, "Future Warfare," 151.

to Clausewitz, combat is the means to subdue the adversary. But he also pointed out that it is not only the destruction of the physical force that is important, but the moral force should also be considered. The insurgency frustrated the Alliance's intentions more on the moral component than the purely physical.

E. INSURGENCY: A PIVOT BETWEEN ESCALATION AND DE-ESCALATION

In 2009, Professors Christopher Daase and Sebastian Schindler in "Clausewitz, Guerillakrieg und Terrorismus. Zur Aktualitat einer missvertandenen Kriegstheorie" remarked that Clausewitz, through his studies on war, not only worked on guerilla warfare (Kleinen Krieg) but also remarked that the boundary between war and warfare was blurred.[326]

What started as inter-state war in Iraq was on the way to a resolution until a guerilla war broke out in the form of insurgency. Guerilla warfare is a pivot between two realms of war (Figure 11). On one side, it expands toward war; on the other side, it deflates toward terrorism and civil disobedience and finally toward peace.

The level of violence was, proportionally to an inter-state war, diminishing but also shifting from the armed forces realm to the civilian realm at the end of Phase III. However, two major factors did not help to stabilize the situation. First was the absence of a concrete plan, akin to Operation Eclipse[327] in WWII, to handle security and a return to normality at the end of the Phase III, which was detrimental to the effort of the Coalition's armed forces. By the time adjustments were done, Iraq went from insurgency to a civil war, where the fault lines were tribal and religious. Second, the way to respond to war versus guerilla warfare differ, not only on operational and strategic levels, with their implications on politics and policies, but also in the way armed forces handle the situation on a tactical level.

---

[326] Christopher Daase and Sebastian Schindler, "Clausewitz, Guerillakrieg und Terrorismus. Zur Aktualitat einer missvertandenen Kriegstheorie," *Politische Viertljahresschrift* 50 (2009), doi:s11615-009-0153-2, 704.
[327] Ledwidge, *Losing Small Wars*, 20.

Figure 11, Continuum of Violence

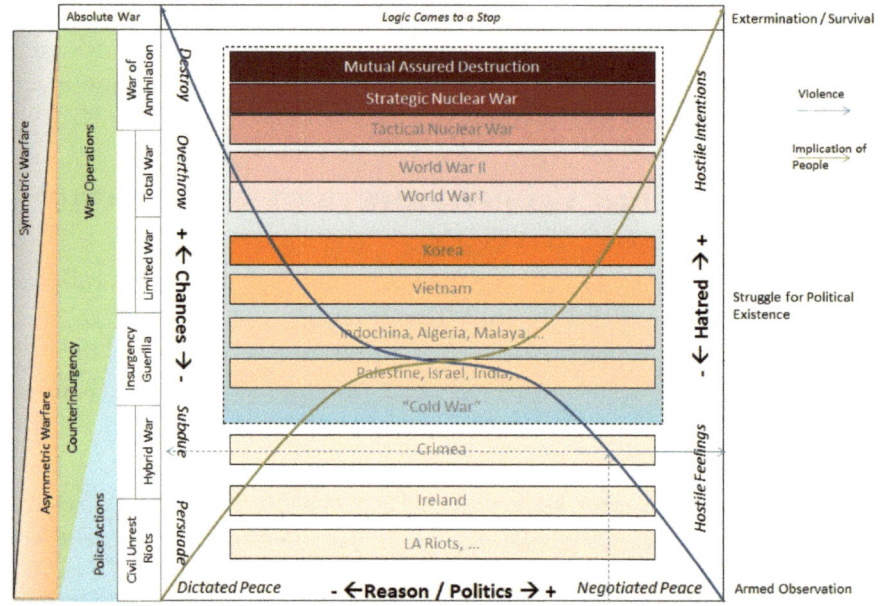

Adapted from Carl von Clausewitz, *On War*, ed. and trans. Michael Howard and Peter Paret (Princeton, NJ: Princeton University Press, 1984); Michael W. Johnson, "Clausewitz on Kosovo: A Monograph" (master's thesis, U.S. Army Command and General Staff College, School of Advanced Military Studies, 2000).

A combat unit that trains for months to storm a house in a combat situation will not handle a house search like a SWAT team or a police officer. The level of violence that may be used by such a combat unit can be exploited as propaganda by the guerillas. Werner Hahlweg remarks:

In this context, he [Clausewitz] also speaks of the possibilities and limitations of terror, arguing that, if one believes 'the enemy would, through the inhuman treatment of the captive insurgents with the death penalty, etc,' demoralize the rebels, we must consider 'repaying atrocity with atrocity, violence with violence! It will be a simple matter for us to outdo the enemy and lead him back into the boundaries of self-control and humanity.'[328]

---

[328] Hahlweg, "Clausewitz and Guerrilla Warfare," 129.

In other words, the game is to downplay physical and moral violence as soon as possible to avoid it being used by the insurgency as a way to recruit new members. Strachan points out that "in American eyes the principle of restraint is now so embedded in some European armies as at time to undermine their military value"[329]; however, restraint may be the solution. Clausewitz explained the spiral of violence, which is the fuel for the guerilla. Iraq and Afghanistan proved him right. Incidents like Abu Ghraib and Haditha only reinforced the guerillas. Proportionality and restraint in the use of force is one key. However, this supposes that two kinds of military units may work in close relations.

An insurgency war needs two types of units within the armed forces to be won—(1) the pure combat unit type, in which the main aim is fighting and which is able to secure a perimeter around an urban area once the main combat operation is ended, and (2) combat units which also act as a reserve to a second type of unit, closer in spirit to a SWAT team in their training and responses. This second type of unit will clean up the urban area of the rest of the bad elements, acting as a police unit in uniform and in spirit. They have to be flexible and trained as police and SWAT more than basic infantry and must act in addition to military police. This second type of units will, in time, turn the responsibility of the security of the urban area to police forces when the level of violence reaches the next pivotal level, that of civil disobedience, and will act as a reserve to police forces. However, these should not be combat units tasked with a new mission, but rather, distinct troops that did not participate in the original fighting.

In short, two strategic errors could have been avoided in Iraq. In his time, Clausewitz already showed how a nation-state losing a war may use guerrilla warfare against an invader and how these guerillas would act and respond to violence. According to Kaplan, Rumsfeld was guilty of this first error because he simply did not believe in the possibility of an insurgency and so did not order the number of troops he was advised to put on the ground. The second error derives

---

[329] Strachan, *Direction of War,"* 130.

from the policy on the use of force; firepower is not always the answer if one wants to minimize the spiral of violence.

F. THE RELATIONSHIP BETWEEN OFFENSE AND DEFENSE IN STRATEGY

The Iraqi war started as an offensive war, which "requires above all a quick, irresistible decision."[330] This decision was realized by the application of Shock and Awe and followed Clausewitz advice against a systematic occupation of useless provinces and followed the "nature of offensive war." In Book VI, Chapter Three, Clausewitz argues that strategic success is directly linked to the capacity of one to exploit tactical victories to shatter the opponent's system. He then lists six main factors for strategic effectiveness: the advantage of terrain, surprise, concentric attack, strengthening the theater, popular support, and exploitation of the moral factor.[331] If the three first factors were easily achieved by the U.S. Armed forces in Iraq and Afghanistan, the same cannot be said of the three remaining ones. Noteworthy is that the three firsts factors correspond to Phase III, while the three lasts fit in the Phase IV.

Clausewitz analyses the factors in terms of the nineteenth century; however, a parallel can be made to the cases examined here. Concerning the fourth factor, strengthening of the theater, the invader is weakened by the fact that he leaves his well-known ground to a newer one. It is now the defender who knows the fields' strengths and weakness and can use it against the invader. In the case of Iraq, weapons caches, knowledge of the local dynamics, and the lack of sensitivity to cultural differences are a few examples that reinforced the defending side.

The fifth factor, the support of the population, encompasses "the effectiveness of the militia, and arming the population. Furthermore, every kind of friction is reduced, and every source of supply is nearer and more abundant [for the defender]."[332] In both Iraq and Afghani-

---

[330] Clausewitz, *On War*, 598.
[331] Ibid., 363.
[332] Clausewitz, *On War*, 365.

stan, this aspect was an important overlooked factor. Both populations were armed, and both the Afghans and Iraqis were effective in the past, against the Russian for the Afghans and Saddam Hussein, respectively. In both cases, the "defending" side, al Qaeda or militias, were able to use the local population as logistics bases. Moreover, the disbandment of the Iraqi Army by ambassador Bremer just gave more trained members and equipment to the local militias. Even if in hindsight it appears that there was no real Iraqi defensive plan to use militias in "stay behind" scenarios, the Pentagon should have planned for a resistance because the probability of its occurrence was itself a risk—as Clausewitz warned, "When a strategic attack is being planned one should from the start give a very close attention to this point—namely the defensive that will follow."[333]

In the case of Iraq, the most overlooked element was the aftermath of the invasion. In the first phase, the coalition was up against one defender, Saddam Hussein, supported by a few members of his tribe. When his regime fell, new defenders arose and competed for power and security for their own tribes. Thus, by ignoring the aftermath of Phase III, the coalition did not recognize the possibility of guerilla warfare sparking along the religious fault lines already cracking, but that had been kept together by Saddam Hussein's iron fist.

Concerning the sixth factor, the moral factors, these are present on both sides. The coalition's armies are generally good at taking care of their own moral factors. However, the lack of understanding of the dynamics of media and in knowing how to interact with it, and with social media in particular, proved to be detrimental over time, especially when coupled with the perceived lack of added security in Iraq and Afghanistan. This may be correlated with the difference in connectivity of both countries. Time is a moral factor which is at the beginning of campaign always overlooked, like the "we will be home for Christmas…" for WWI. If "war serves the purpose of the defense more than of the aggressor,"[334] this is also true for the guerilla warfare which "defends" its own field, and it was best described by the first slide from the "council of colonels" brief to General Peter Pace:

---

[333] Ibid.
[334] Clausewitz, *On War*, 370.

"We are losing because we are not winning. And we are running out of time."[335] The fact that the invader is running out of time is an advantage for the guerilla warfare, which wins by not losing. With respect to the number of guerilla conflicts in which America has intervened openly or covertly around the world in the past century, it is still puzzling that, despite warnings, the decision-makers at the political level did not admit the possibility of a long, protracted conflict in either Afghanistan or Iraq.

With the passing of time, war affects the political realm and forces it to change its policies because of widespread discontent or other pressure from the people. This was true for Vietnam and will be true also for the future wars. Long wars are not suited for democratic countries, as General Marshall warned: "A democracy cannot fight a Seven Years War."[336] Thus, the scope of war should be limited, with achievable goals for the armed forces. The core of the problem resides in the strategic views of the decision-making actors. Colonel Gentile stated,

Our senior leaders could have discerned early the folly of trying to build Afghanistan into a modern state overnight and would have deduced that the core policy goal of destroying al Qaeda could have been done by a much smaller force concentrated against the few remaining al Qaeda left after the Taliban had been removed in early 2002. Unfortunately, Americans strategy has failed in Afghanistan (and Iraq) because it was founded on an illusion – that American style counterinsurgency could win Muslim hearts and minds at gun-point and create viable nation-states on the Western model virtually from scratch in a short time.[337]

Gentile was making a point that the goals of the wars were blurred and thus no coherent strategy could eventuate in the face of the dual problems of resistance in the two nations. The aim was to destroy the al Qaeda terror network, but over time, it transformed itself into a mission of nation-building in Afghanistan, and a regime change from a tyrannical regime to a democratic state, also implying a goal of na-

---

[335] Cited in Kaplan, *Insurgents*, 231.
[336] Paret, Craig, and Gilbert, *Makers of Modern Strategy*, 681.
[337] Gentile, *Wrong Turn*, 135.

tion-building activities, with an approach based on a Western ideology and way of life, which is not the cultural background of the targeted countries.

Despite all claims to the contrary, the Global War on Terror is not a strategy, and not even a policy. Clausewitz warns not to go to war without knowing the goal of the war, knowing how to conduct the war, and knowing the political purpose and its operational objectives.[338] The U.S. choice to include Iraq in the Global War on Terror was an error for numerous reasons. First, an action against terrorism cannot be waged on a global scale with the same forces and rules around the globe; strategy and operations have to be tailored to fit the local conditions, and Afghanistan is not Iraq. Second, the name itself—Global War on Terror—is targeting a way of fighting and not an actual actor; there is almost no possibility for defining measurable, achievable goals for the armed forces. However, if the armed forces fought a war against al Qaeda, the goal would be clearer and could be measured. Third, the Global War on Terror is bound up with Western ideology. No short war can be fought against an ideology. The Cold War was an ideological war, but it was fought and won based on such tangible assets as economy, and it took decades to win it. Ideology was the background, not the medium, used to fight a confusing conflict that always threatened to end in total catastrophe.

Fourth, the Afghanistan operation started as separate from Iraq in all possible relations. Al Qaeda was in the aftermath of September 11, a legitimate target and recognized as such by the vast majority of the world; Iraq was not. Colin Powell, then U.S. secretary of state, tried hard to sell the risk of Iraqi weapons of mass destruction (WMDs) as a just cause. If the WMDs were such a worry for America, why did the CIA have so "little concrete information"[339] on the 946 sites? By trying to hit multiple targets with the same war, it not only used more resources, but it confused the overall U.S. strategy. From the destruction of the Taliban and al Qaeda to a regime change in Iraq and nation-building in two countries, there was no possibility of bringing it all under the same Global War on Terror from the start. In the case

---

[338] Clausewitz, *On War*, 579.

[339] Gordon and Trainor, *Cobra II,* 92.

of Afghanistan, it was viewed as police action against terrorists, which was the actual goal. No one was expecting an "absolute form of war," with the only option being a "final victory."[340] In Iraq, the build-up and the expectation of the U.S. military-political decision-maker was closer to the absolute form of war. In the end, the result was that the final victory never materialized. The media and the population at home was waiting for it and did not understand, nor did anyone explain, that the two types of war that America was in, were a lesser form of war, a limited war, in which "all that counts is the total score, and each separate result makes its contribution toward this total."[341] In other words, Afghanistan and Iraq should have been fought under separate "wars" and never have been linked in any form; the "global" is partially responsible for the unwanted outcomes.

In Afghanistan, the goal was to remove the Taliban and al Qaeda. This could have been done without nation-building. In Iraq, the toppling of Saddam Hussein was only one battle, not the end of the war. As a regime change was announced, the obvious end of the war would have been a peace agreement with a new regime operating in a safe and secure environment. Simpson deduced "if force is to have political utility, one needs to understand the nature of the problem on its own terms, not through dogmatically applied ideological or doctrinal lenses."[342] The problem with the Global War on Terror was the generalization of the aim which "fails to understand one's environment in its own political terms, [thus] one does not know what political effect one will have."[343] This discrepancy will eventually be corrected on the *National Strategy for Counterterrorism* in June 2011: "The United States deliberately uses the word 'war' to describe our relentless campaign against al-Qa'ida. However, this Administration has made it clear that we are not at war with the tactic of terrorism or the religion of Islam. We are at war with a specific organization—al-

---

[340] Clausewitz, *On War*, 582.
[341] Ibid.
[342] Simpson, *War from the Ground Up*, 103.
[343] Ibid.

Qa'ida."344 However, the resulting series of half measures in between was a butchered political result of both conflicts in Afghanistan and Iraq. The misconception reflected by the highest level of the politic decision-making at the beginning of these two conflicts, and more specifically in Iraq, on which kind of war they were on the verge of entering was important until the "surge," as Kaplan pointed out: "the American authorities still seemed in denial over the nature and scope of the problem."345

In both cases, the nation-building piece of the campaign came after the start of military operations. Nation-building is a long process, which may span over generations, difficult enough in more peaceful conditions like in Kosovo or Bosnia, in which Europe, along with the United States, had been active since the end of the last century. Moreover, the Balkan states were proportionally more advanced than Afghanistan and almost similar in development to Iraq. There was no reason to suppose it would go faster with the two latter countries, especially as they were not embracing Western mindsets or values, which were present in the Balkans to start with.

War is won when the enemy is defeated. In the cases of Afghanistan and Iraq, the following assertion should be made: war is won when the enemies are defeated; and Clausewitz would have added, "but what exactly does 'defeat' signify?"346 There is a discrepancy between Clausewitz's interpretation of the defeat and Iraq after the fall of Saddam's regime or Afghanistan. Clausewitz offers three general possibilities to defeat the enemy: destruction of the army, seizure of the capital, or the delivery of an effective blow against his principal ally.347 In the case of the Taliban and al Qaeda, and for the militias in Iraq, Clausewitz's three possibilities to defeat an enemy would have to be summarized as follows: destruction of its forces, seizure of its

---

344 President of the United States, "National Strategy for Counterterrorism" (Washington, DC: The White House, June 28, 2011), https://www.whitehouse.gov/sites/default/files/counterterrorism_strategy.pdf.
345 Kaplan, *Insurgents*, 167.
346 Clausewitz, *On War*, 595.
347 Ibid., 596.

bases, and destruction of its allies. This is also true if there is more than one enemy.

Gentile reported that the fight against al Qaeda in Afghanistan was problematic because al Qaeda did not operate with constancy. Clausewitz argues that the more the enemies are in an alliance instead of acting as independent actors, the more they can be regarded as one opponent.[348] This is what was done in Afghanistan as well as in Iraq. They were regarded as one opponent until late in the conflicts because it was assumed they had an alliance, in the way Western armed forces understood alliances. In reality, it was a loose aggregation of "armed groups" with caveats, not an alliance.[349] Thus, in the words of Clausewitz, when centers of gravity cannot be fused in one, one should "act as if there were two wars or even more, each with its own object."[350] Not only does this view require "adequate" forces, but "we must be certain our political position is so secure that this success will not bring further enemies against us who could force us immediately to abandon our efforts against our first opponent."[351]

What Clausewitz did not have during his life is global connectivity. Because of connectivity, Simpson postulates that "war today is in the process of undergoing another evolution in response to social and political conditions, namely the speed and interconnectivity associated with contemporary globalization and the information revolution."[352] Unlike van Creveld, Simpson stresses an *evolution,* which concurs with Clausewitz's views on the use of technologies by armies,[353] to which one has to adapt, not a *revolution* in warfare.

One may disagree with Simpson's suggestion that war itself is undergoing the transformation process, but leaders in charge of the conduct of the war have to understand how to use those news tools efficiently toward populations which are not from the same culture and do not aspire to the same "way of life," to support combat opera-

---

[348] Clausewitz, *On War*, 596.
[349] Simpson, *War from the Ground Up*, 102.
[350] Clausewitz, *On War*, 597
[351] Clausewitz, *On War*, 597
[352] Simpson, *War from the Ground Up*, 228.
[353] Clausewitz, *On War*, 75.

tions adequately. Simpson demonstrates that connectivity and the use of narratives are powerful if well used. Democratic states are weaker in the use of narrative than groups such has al Qaeda and its affiliates, mainly because of legal self-imposed constraints, in Clausewitz's view.[354]

Connectivity permits the broadcasting of another narrative of what is going on on the ground and appeals to other fragments of societies farther away from the battlefield: "Counterinsurgency is a competition with the insurgent for the right to win the hearts [and] minds."[355] The cultural and political misunderstanding of Western states toward the East has proven to be detrimental in the short term. The rise of groups such as the Islamic State of Iraq and ash-Sham (ISIS) and its further denominations have proved Simpson right in his analysis, if, as Simpson says, in a Clausewitzian world, "the core strategic audiences of the conflict are to be found within the side themselves."[356] One shall not forget that with connectivity, other audiences outside the two or more camps are yet relevant. This extension of the original core audiences' appeal for another message is directed to the new fringes to convince them of the goals of the war.

In Afghanistan, for instance, one of the problems was that the Western nations referred to it as a unitary land with a central government. However, every province in Afghanistan should have been treated as a country because of its tribal fractioning, in which the central government is the tribe leader. In such an approach, Clausewitz is relevant. In Clausewitz's view, one can only fail if Afghanistan is considered as a single unified country because it is not what it is in reality at the time; the central government was not recognized by all provinces. This highly dynamic environment for decision-making necessitates a high coordination of all assets until a central government is recognized.[357]

Such an environment demands adequate counterinsurgency *tactics*, tailored for the specific environment. "The requirement of strategic

---

[354] Ibid.
[355] Kaplan, *Insurgents*, 175.
[356] Simpson, *War from the Ground Up*, 228.
[357] Ibid., 230.

narrative to bind its audience is crucial,"[358] as Simpson says, but there is a double-edged sword. First, the education of the masses sharpened the narrative as everyone interpreted the message with his own bias. Second, coupled with the availability of information (globalization), the narrative has to be free of lies to be persuasive. If two totally different narratives are found, educated masses will start to doubt what is said. This is the danger of the digitized world. Narratives must be synchronized with what may be seen, read, or watched on film.

People in Iraq or Afghanistan may want both peace and more liberty. However, as General Pete W. Chiarelli asked, "What if they just don't want what we want?"[359] Not only may they not want it our way, but as Gentile remarks, the overall structure of their society may not be ready for a change "after ten years of nation building, something resembling democracy in the Hindu Kush will take generations and generations to create."[360] Thus, keeping the political and military aims of the war limited at the start may help to avoid long conflicts that democracies cannot win because the population's discontent overtime will only reinforce, directly or indirectly, the guerrilla side.

Clausewitz sees the use of guerilla warfare at the periphery of the main battle: "The operations of the guerrilla units, whether militia or bands of inhabitants, should always take place just outside the theater of war where the enemy forces do not appear in strength, on the 'edges.'"[361] In other words, guerilla is a part of a "larger scale" war; however, it may not be seen as such as recent cases plainly suggest. The question, specifically in the case of Iraq, is, where is the real war, that is, the center of gravity; did Iraq become a proxy war when the Saddam Hussein regime fell?

In his Book Six, Chapter Six, Clausewitz explains the relationship between the militias and the concept of defense and also stresses the "defender's allies" as "his ultimate source of support."[362] Moreover,

---

[358] Ibid., 117.
[359] Kaplan, *Insurgents*, 222.
[360] Gentile, *Wrong Turn*, 114.
[361] Hahlweg, "Clausewitz and Guerrilla Warfare," 131.
[362] Clausewitz, *On War*, 373.

an ally is not to be understood as a direct ally, but one "who [has] a substantial interest in maintaining the integrity of their ally's country."[363] The coalition forces did not recognize early enough the rise of the sectarian violence in Iraq after the fall of the regime and misinterpreted it as a resistance against the coalition and its effort of "liberating Iraq." What could have happened was the emergence of a proxy war between Iran and the United States through militias. The Iranians' end goals may not have been to directly support religious sectarian conflict, but by fueling it and by staying outside, it certainly helped to show Iran as a regional power and put pressure on the United States to solve Iranian interest outside the sectarian realm.

From past experience, it was foreseeable that the coalition would enter Iraq and push the Iraqi army within the borders of its country. Hannah Arendt also demonstrates in *On Violence,* that "if a foreign conqueror is confronted by an impotent government and by a nation unused to the exercise of political power, it is easy for him to achieve such domination."[364] Saddam Hussein's regime, being a unique ruling party system, did not prepare the state apparatus to take over and be independent of its leader. The fall of Saddam Hussein's regime followed by the de-Ba'athification of the state apparatus resulted in the destruction of the state's power and nobody in power outside the party was able to step in and take responsibility for Iraq in a coherent effort from the start. Iraq did not have the same history of liberalism as Germany had prior to the 1940s; the de-Nazification was possible because Germany's recent past allowed it. For the sectarian leaders in Iraq, the aim of their war was to gain power to assert themselves, and in some respect, to protect their communities from others. Their aim fulfilled Maslow's Pyramid of Needs, especially when the strong central power had vanished and the occupation powers were not able to provide basic security to all. Arendt argues that "where power has disintegrated, revolutions are possible, but not necessary."[365]

In the Iraqi case, the militias did not pursue revolution; they wanted to reassert power. Arendt also recognizes that "power is in-

---

[363] Ibid.
[364] Arendt, *On Violence,* 52.
[365] Ibid., 49.

deed of the essence of all government, but violence is not," for no government can survive based on violence only.[366] By the beginning of the invasion, the lack of a good strategy regarding the stabilization phase[367] allowed violence to take over the state's residual power and permitted its destruction; this became especially true when Presidential Envoy Bremer unilaterally disbanded the Iraqi army, the last available resort to implement some degree of security in the country by a local authority.

Tactical victories can be achieved with violence, but without power, no strategic peace can be reached, because every side will pay a high price to achieve fewer stable results and, according to Arendt, power never grows out of violence.[368] When power is eroded by violence, the last remaining possibility to maintain domination is terror as a "form of government that comes into being when violence, having destroyed all power, does not abdicate, but on the contrary, remains in full control. … Every kind of organized opposition must disappear before the full force of terror can be let loose."[369] The lack of a plan for stabilization, the premature de-Ba'athification of Iraq and the disbandment of the Iraqi army permitted the erosion of power, which authorized the apparition of sectarian violence, which in turn opened the gates to terrorism. Kaplan explains it well:

The problem was that in some cases … the insurgency was the population or an important segment of it. If, as the manual stated, a purely military solution isn't possible, if these kinds of wars usually end with a political negotiation, this poses a problem.[370]

When the insurgency started, the coalition forces were an enemy to any sectarian factions because they stood between targets and reduced the liberty of action of the factions to go at each other's throats to assert power over the other. In such a situation, the factions had to

---

[366] Ibid., 50–51.
[367] Bolger, *Why We Lost*, 118.
[368] Arendt, *On Violence*, 50–51.
[369] Arendt, *On Violence*, 55.
[370] Kaplan, *Insurgents*, 159.

rely on some form of resistance to survive and on guerilla warfare to regain some degree of liberty of action.

In Book Six, Chapter Eight, Clausewitz analyzes four types of resistance. In all cases, the defender has the advantage. Logically, when the defender is outnumbered, the logic is to "withdraw to the interior of the country and resist there … the simplest and most outstanding example would be the case in which the defender is able to leave one or more fortresses behind, which the attacker must invest or besiege."[371] In the case of Iraq and Afghanistan, the fourth case is more interesting to analyze because it is the one that is "particularly effective in weakening the enemy."[372] Clausewitz explains the use of fortresses to weaken the adversary. Of course, there are no more fortresses today; however, the parallel with cities like Basra, Tikrit, or Mosul may be explored. Kilcullen also refers to "garrison community" to "describe the informal system of security and order that have emerged in marginalized urban settlements,"[373] similar in many ways to the old concept of a military garrison in charge of a sector. It may not have been a fortress in the common view but it played the same role, a focal point with "two distinct elements, one active and one passive."[374] The active part is the defender or rebels, and the passive part being the protection through anonymity that the city by its size, gives the rebels.

This combination draws a huge amount of forces to stabilize or "seize" such a "fortress" and therefore weakens the situation of the coalition in the rest of the country; the result was "obvious that it will weaken his [the invader's] forces and provide an opportunity for the attack by the defender at a point where he has the upper hand."[375] First, the city draws forces to secure; second, once inside, the invader's freedom of movement is reduced; and third, he is more exposed than before to the defender,[376] making this a perfect "focal

---

[371] Clausewitz, *On War*, 381.
[372] Ibid., 382.
[373] Kilcullen, *Out of Mountains*, 89.
[374] Clausewitz, *On War*, 394.
[375] Ibid., 381.
[376] Ibid., 397.

point of a general insurrection."[377] Today's cities are yesterday's fortresses; urbanization is one of the four factors that will challenge armed forces in David Kilcullen's views of the future of warfare in his last book, *Out of the Mountains*.[378]

Fighting in such situations will also cost the guerrilla side—with time, it will be weakened; the remaining question is, who will be weakened first? The time factor elapses in a relative and different way for each side. For the invader, as losses grow and the effort seems to be ineffective at first, his moral may decline. The defender side is betting on lower losses at first and gaining moral support from the inhabitants to replenish his forces with time. Time is on the side of guerillas because they only have to make sure not to be defeated to win. As Clausewitz argues, when the defender cannot defend the country anymore and retreats, his aim will change from protection of the country to a "favorable peace."[379] This is what happened in Iraq after the fall of the regime during the "Anbar Awaking." For some militias, a favorable peace was possible; concessions were made by the militias as well as by the coalition, giving credit to Gentile's observations that "sometimes, in a war that involves limited policy aims, there may well be alternative to [total] victory."[380] The problem was more due to prior bold statements draped in Western ideology made by political decision-makers at a strategic level, which impaired possible agreements at the operational or tactical levels.

Resistance, as Clausewitz points out, by its nature will not permit a major counteroffensive from the invader. Clausewitz complains that previous commanders did not report enough of their experiences on this not-very-common way of war and therefore an in-depth analysis is not possible. However, he sees two options at a strategic level: once one has lost the war, the choices are to try to come to a better peace agreement or to help in the main battle,[381] such as the French Resistance in support of D-Day in 1944. Resistance may have different

---

[377] Ibid., 399.
[378] Kilcullen, *Out of Mountains*.
[379] Clausewitz, *On War*, 471.
[380] Gentile, *Wrong Turn*, 118.
[381] Clausewitz, *On War*, 483.

outcomes and Clausewitz did not foresee effective resistance on a larger scale as being possible outside of Russia, because of the need for space to be efficient.[382] However, resistance in diverse conflicts has proven to be possible in smaller areas than Russia; Afghanistan and Iraq proved to be large enough.

Clausewitz makes an interesting point in his Book Six, Chapter Twenty-Six, listing five criteria that favor the resistance movement. They are summarized in Table 2 and compared with other theaters of war. These four countries differ in sizes and climate but were all successful in some way in their resistances.

Clausewitz's description on how militias and rebels have to be used in order to be efficient is well known and proved to be efficient in all the four countries in the table. However, if Clausewitz foresaw such usage of militias at a country level, it did not encompass the atomization of such militias as seen with Iraq or Afghanistan. Nonetheless, if one can find the trinity of those militias, Clausewitz's principles still apply. As efficient as it can be, such insurgencies can also be defeated;[383] this was the effort of the proponents of COIN more or less after the year 2005.

---

[382] Ibid., 480. This is due to the fact that he primarily analyzed only European wars and no other theater during his lifetime. Safe haven can also be found where borders are porous (e.g., Pakistan in the case of Afghanistan, which allows the use of a "considerable region" in a Clausewitzian point of view.)

[383] Clausewitz, *On War*, 481.

Table 2: Clausewitz's Conditions for Effectiveness of a General Uprising

Clausewitz's conditions for effectiveness of a general uprising	Kosovo	Vietnam	Afghanistan	Iraq
1. The war must be fought in the interior of the country.	Y	Y	Y	Y
2. It must not be decided by a single stroke of the enemy.	Y	Y	Y	Y
3. The theater of operations must constitute a "considerable region."	N	Y	Y	Y
4. The national character must be suited to this type of armed confrontation.	Y Family (clans)	Y	Y Tribal	Y Tribal
5. The terrain must be rough and inaccessible because of mountains, forests, swamps, or "the local methods of cultivation."	Y	Y	Y	Y

As Porch remarks, "campaigns of counterinsurgency conducted by outsiders often fail because they create legitimacy gaps that are exploited by insurgents."[384] This gap is often to be found in the political realm, expressed first in their incapacity to deliver security and justice. Clausewitz explains why such insurgency was not possible under the reign of Saddam Hussein: "National uprising cannot maintain itself where the atmosphere is too full of danger."[385] The way out may rest on an understanding of the "trinity." According to Gordon, the U.S. political-military level did not understand "the actual structure of po-

---

[384] Porch, *Counterinsurgency*, 338.
[385] Clausewitz, *On War*, 482.

litical power in Iraq,"³⁸⁶ neither the kind of enemy fought once the regime fell, which was a decentralized one.³⁸⁷

This reinforces the analysis of Captain Brett Friedmann in his article "Creeping Death,"³⁸⁸ published in February 2014 in the *Military Review*. Friedmann argues that COIN specialists have ignored Clausewitz's trinity leading to a known result. His analysis argues for a COIN approach along the trinity and neither "population-centric" or "enemy-centric": "The trinity's nodes must be seized and the insurgents' system flooded. Insurgencies die through suffocation."³⁸⁹ Thus, Friedmann not only links counterinsurgency to a national-level mission and not just a purely military one, but also integrates John Boyd in the effort. Friedmann's idea is to outrun the adversary OODA loops base on the adversary's inability to keep his own trinity untouched.

The classical Clausewitz expert, Hahlweg, remarks that "guerrilla war can only be understood in the larger political-strategic context. As part of a general strategy, it will fully develop its potential strength;"³⁹⁰ hence, the solution as to be political-strategic first and military second. As Simpson remarks, "an operational approach must connect back to its political purpose, or risk that self-referencing military logic drive a war much further than political utility,"³⁹¹ which echoes Clausewitz in his Book Eight: "whenever this occurs ... the many links that connect the two elements are destroyed and we are left with something pointless and devoid of sense."³⁹² If Clausewitz, and history, make it clear that in every war, policies play a role, the primacy of the political realm over the military realm is established.

---

³⁸⁶ Gordon and Trainor, *Cobra II*, 573.

³⁸⁷ Ibid.

³⁸⁸ Captain Brett Friedmann, "Creeping Death," *Military Review* (January–February 2014), 83.

³⁸⁹ Friedmann, "Creeping Death," 85.

³⁹⁰ Hahlweg, "Clausewitz and Guerrilla Warfare," 132–33.

³⁹¹ Simpson, *War from the Ground Up*, 137.

³⁹² Clausewitz, *On War*, 605.

However, in the recent past, with Iraq and Afghanistan, the political realm misunderstood Clausewitz, as did the military realm, by claiming that only Jomini was right. Clausewitz claims that policy rules over the military; the use of force is a political act to achieve a political aim. "If war is part of policy, policy will determine its character."[393] But the political realm's prerogative stops there: "Policy, of course, will not extend its influence to operational details ... but they are the most influential in the planning of war, of the campaign, and often even of the battle."[394] The micromanagement under Rumsfeld went against this concept, and needless to say against Jomini's views.

What is policy? "The aim of policy is to unify and reconcile all aspects of internal administration as well as of spiritual values. ... we can only treat policy as representative of all interests of the community."[395] Policy is thus the base of the national strategy on which war plans are established subordinating the military realm to the political. It also entails the coordination factor in regards to the DIME realms. If "war is simply a continuation of the political intercourse, with the addition of other means,"[396] then strategy is a two-way bridge, as described by Simpson, Strachan, Gentile, and confirmed by General Zinni.[397]

Clausewitz's deductions focused on war between states; however, these tenets are still true if during the analysis of a conflict (e.g., Afghanistan), planners take the time to admit that in absence of a central government, they have to treat each provincial government as the counterpart to whom the military campaign is aimed at. Such admission leads to a complex, dynamic military environment, which cannot by itself resolve all problems without a continuous link with the national strategy. This link, as Simpson said, is a two-way bridge. In a dynamic information society, it requires a constant dialogue between the operational level and the national strategy level. The dynamic is such in the globalized world that delay may impair sound judgments

---

[393] Ibid., 606.
[394] Clausewitz, *On War*, 606.
[395] Ibid., 605.
[396] Ibid.
[397] Zinni and Koltz, *Before First Shots Are Fired*, 105.

and plead for a political decision-making representative on the side of the operational level in the theater, or at least that the guidance given allows enough latitude to the military decision-making to reach, when needed, the immediate decision in the frame given by its political leaders.

In such fragmented societies, a Manichean view of the world is seldom possible or useful. Another consideration is that Clausewitz's realm is war, and thus does not apply to nation-building, in which Machiavelli may be more relevant, as he wrote *Prince*, extensively studied by Clausewitz,[398] during a troubled time of fragmented societies. Western states have to avoid such declarations in black or white terms and focus on goals that can be seen in shades of gray, at least during the nation-building phase. There are some values that are non-negotiable; however, Western states have to also be realistic and accept a step-by-step negotiating process rather than an all-or-nothing negotiation.

In non-state conflicts, the first important step is to build trust to go forward. However, sometimes the ally of yesterday is today's enemy, and may be tomorrow's friend. In order to not alienate these possibilities, small steps are needed in the same way that time is needed. Time plays a central role in war. The tempo has to be on the invader's side if he wants to prevail. But when combat operations are ended, if the real strategic-political goal is stability, nation-building has to be part of the overall plan. Nation-building by its essence is a long and costly process, as shown throughout history in Germany, Japan, Korea, Bosnia, Kosovo, and other places. History equally shows that the more fragmented a country is in its society (ethnicity, religion, etc.), the longer the investment of time to reach state-wide stability. If Western states are not ready to commit to a multi-generation-long investment, the political-strategic goal should be clearly defined as ending with the conclusion of the combat operation and with the withdrawal.

This is why, militarily, the first Persian Gulf was a success and not the second; the first time there was no nation-building. However, for

---

[398] Peter Paret, "Machiavelli, Fichte, and Clausewitz in the Labyrinth of German Idealism," manuscript, May 18, 2015, received from Prof. Donald Abenheim.

nation-building to work, trust and security must be the precondition to a political settlement.[399] Situations from Iraq and Afghanistan have demonstrated that if security was a problem, establishing trust was a greater problem. History had a role, as demonstrated by the British in Basora, but also the lack of coordination at the national level between the DIME realm and military actions at the operational level, which had repercussions at the tactical level. This dichotomy created a cycle of mistrust, which fueled the insurgency.

This cycle started by an absence of a clear top-down coordinated strategy, not only in the DIME realm, but also interagency-wise. In the absence of strategy, units try to solve problems as they can by isolated actions. When those actions reach the higher level, they are discarded (for various reasons, such as a group helping at the tactical level is not supporting women's rights, for example). As a result, higher levels undo previous promises from the tactical units, fueling the narrative of the insurgency along the lines of "you see, they do not hold their words; we cannot trust them." Depending on the tactical costs, this produces new recruits for insurgency or at least a higher level of mistrust between the population and the coalition. As tactical units rotate frequently, the locals may not forget the previous reality or perceived betrayal of the departing unit. The new units do not understand why its "strategy" does not work and try to change the approach, resulting in a strategy that is even less coordinated with the upper level.[400] This is one example of misunderstanding due to a lack in policy.[401]

As a result, "policy could make demands on war which war could not fulfill."[402] Clausewitz concludes that "at the highest level the art

---

[399] Kaplan, *Insurgents,* 198.

[400] Kaplan, *Insurgents,* 186, but also 246, 247, 248, 279, 280–81, 321.

[401] This also point to the problem of rotation of units in war. During WWI and WWII there was no such high tempo in rotation. Larger wars with broader problems were solved in a lesser amount of time. This trend started with the Vietnam War and continues today with known results. It may be far-reaching to say that high tempo rotation is the cause of unfinished war and it is not the theme of this dissertation. However, the linkage would be interesting to investigate. In the meantime, it speaks for a higher coordination of policy and action from the top to the bottom.

[402] Clausewitz, *On War,* 607.

of war turns into policy"[403] and disregards a "purely military"[404] option at this level as much as he discards the idea that a general should give "*purely military advice*"[405] to its government. This is the two-way bridge that was missing in Afghanistan and Iraq, according to General Zinni,[406] Kaplan, Strachan, Simpson, and Gentile.

In this demonstration, Clausewitz does not preach for an apolitical priesthood of the military person. The use of the army is subordinate to the politic; the generals have to explain the political consequences of military actions; the army fights to reach military objectives with political significances; but the soldier, as a citizen, can vote as he wants. Now, every soldier applies this as he himself sees fit. Eisenhower, MacArthur, or Pershing had different approaches.

For John Nagl, "counterinsurgency is not just thinking man's warfare—it is the graduate level of war,"[407] and Etienne de Durand posits that "[Colonel] Lacheroy begins with the misunderstood originality and effectiveness of revolutionary warfare, which is not small war or guerilla warfare under another name, but the truest and most accomplished form of total war."[408] Haleweg, on his side, is persuaded that

> an investigation of the nature, function, possibilities, and limitations of guerrilla warfare either in history or in the present day—cannot ignore Clausewitz. His work *On War* may contribute to the further development of a modern, comprehensive, and philosophically-founded theory of guerrilla warfare.[409]

Guerilla or insurgency is distinct from pure terrorism by its need to use offense and defense in a limited manner to be efficient over time. Terrorism is only hit and run. Defense is only to avoid capture. Insur-

---

[403] Ibid.

[404] Ibid.

[405] Ibid.

[406] Zinni and Koltz, *Before First Shots Are Fired*, 105.

[407] Nagl, as cited in Kaplan, *Insurgents*, 164.

[408] Étienne de Durand, "France," in *Understanding Counterinsurgency: Doctrine, Operations, and Challenges*, eds. Thomas Rid and Thomas Keaney (London and New York: Routledge, 2010), 17.

[409] Hahlweg, "Clausewitz and Guerrilla Warfare," 132–33.

gency needs, on one hand, territories to survive and grow; thus, they need to defend their territories. But on the other hand, the insurgents need to pressure their adversary to divert its efforts over other, less important, territories to attack their adversary and show its weakness. In this respect insurgent follow a limited aims in offense and defense. In an offensive war, insurgents seek the occupation of part of the territory to gain resources. This is a viable option for guerillas. It gives more leverage for negotiations and diverts adversary assets from their main task in order to resize those territories.[410] In the limited aim for a defensive war, "If we considered the relative exhaustion of forces on both sides, the defender is at a disadvantage."[411] If the guerilla fighter cannot significantly weaken the attacker rapidly, overtime, the guerilla weakens quicker. However, Clausewitz remarksthat "the fatigue of the stronger has often brought about peace."[412] This is based on the factor of time. The guerilla fighter has to use time to defeat Goliath and bet on change in the political climate; as Clausewitz suggests, either the guerilla fighters gain new allies or his enemy's allies start to desert, tipping the balance of power in the other direction. In the case of Afghanistan and Iraq, both options applied.

G. A WAR PLAN DESIGNED FOR THE TOTAL DEFEAT OF THE ENEMY

Clausewitz points out two principles to achieve such a plan: concentration and speed. This requires defining the center of gravity that has to be destroyed. In physics, there is only one center of gravity for a physical object. The wording "center of gravity" led to a misunderstanding in the planning. In the original manuscript, Clausewitz refers to *Schwerpunkt*, which translates better to "point of effort" or "focal point." One can argue back and forth on the accuracy of the translation, but one has to recognize that today a state's complex system does not offer a single point to attack in order to paralyze the whole state. This is the whole *raison d'être* of redundancy of systems of control and command in a state. Thus, the relationship to the physical

---

[410] Clausewitz, *On War*, 611.
[411] Ibid., 613.
[412] Ibid.

description can be misleading. With this translation, one allows multiple "point of efforts" to be attacked in the complex systems of today. In the normal PMESII analysis of a state, every system has different nodes, which once destroyed, paralyze a part of the system, and finally its whole. Even when overlapping, complex systems do not give only one single center of gravity.

The killing of Osama bin Laden has proven that bin Laden was not *the* center of gravity for al Qaeda; al Qaeda did not collapse, but bin Laden was certainly one of the nodes, which necessitated a specific effort to be made. Clausewitz tries to diminish the number of those "Schwerpünkte" to a single one; however, he recognize that due to some parameters described in Book Eight, Chapter Nine, it is not always feasible. The closer to the combat, the easier it is to find only one center of gravity; but at a strategic level, a state has multiple centers of gravity. This is also true if the enemy is not a single entity. It is easier to define the center of gravity of the U.S. Army as being its logistical dependency than to define a single center of gravity for the Global War on Terror; but even there, what installation should be whipped out to stop cold the U.S. armed forces at once? Clausewitz's center of gravity must be seen as a neuralgic point in the subsystem of the state. However, Clausewitz said "we hold, moreover, that the plan of operations should have this tendency even when the enemy's whole resistance cannot be reduced to a single center of gravity and when, as we have once put it, two almost wholly separate wars have to be fought simultaneously,"[413] this tendency being "to keep each minor operation as subordinate as possible."[414] This is the unity of command, which must be maintained.

In Iraq, the two simultaneous wars were nothing but Phase III and Phase IV. Two types of engagements should have been planned and executed almost simultaneously, but under the same higher command. Gray also sees the strategic value of that for the coordination of efforts along the state's actors regarding the use of national pow-

---

[413] Clausewitz, *On War*, 623.
[414] Ibid.

ers, but he sees it more "theoretical than practical"[415] due to the difference of reaction in time of the PMESII. However, in order to win, this has to be done practically. Some actions may have to be implemented earlier than others to achieve their effects at the right moment to support military action. This is strategic planning.

If in a normal war, one tends to achieve a "concentric attack," in an insurgency or guerilla war, a "divided attack" may be necessary.[416] This reflection is based on the fact that insurgency, by its nature, tends to not concentrate its forces. Divided attack may also be translated today as attacks on multiple nodes of the complex system of the insurgency faced. This led to the question of the concentration of forces or mass. Colin S. Gray points out that "the idea that mass really meant [is] the 'massing of effect' not forces;"[417] in other words, it is to concentrate enough means of the right quality to achieve the desired effect at the right time in the right space. This can be a division or just a sniper team—the size is not the principal matter. This is also true for the insurgency; proportional to their seizure, a team with a bomb is a concentration of mass.

The second principle is speed. "Speed and impetus are its [initial surprise] strongest elements and are usually indispensable if we are to defeat the enemy."[418] Today, this remains true at an operational level. However, at a strategic level, surprise cannot easily be achieved and certainly not with operations like in Afghanistan and Iraq due to the sheer amount of means to be readied. Al Qaeda achieved a strategic surprise with far fewer means on September 11, but they were not surprised by the aftermath. That is to say, speed is an operational element, not a strategic one. An assault may be timed, not a war.

If a state decided to enter a war, it should aim for a long commitment and plan accordingly. This implies a broader mobilization to call

---

[415] Colin S. Gray, "Principles of War or Principles of Battle?" in *Rethinking the Principles of War*, ed. McIvor, Anthony (Annapolis, MD: Naval Institute Press, 2005), 67.
[416] Clausewitz, *On War*, 619.
[417] Gray, "Principles of War," 66.
[418] Clausewitz, *On War*, 624.

the reserves and start the training for war, with all of its consequences, because as Clausewitz remarks:

Once a major victory is achieved there must be no talk of rest, of breathing space, of reviewing the position or consolidating and so forth, but only of the pursuit, going for the enemy again if necessary, seizing his capital, attacking his reserves and anything else that might give his country aid and comfort.[419]

An adequate mobilization of comprehensive resources can only be done through accurate intelligence work. This intelligence must not only occur on the military level because danger can also come from history, religion, and neighborhood, to cite a few of the possibilities. Clausewitz remarks that

to discover how much of our resources must be mobilized for war we must first examine our own political aim and that of the enemy. We must gauge the strength and the situation of the opposing state. We must gauge the character and abilities of its government and people and to do the same in regard to our own. Finally, we must evaluate the political sympathies of other states and effect the war may have on them.[420]

The inadequacy of forces after Phase III and the absence of a plan for Phase IV achieved exactly the opposite of a total victory. The major victory was not exploited by faulty policitics back in the Pentagon: the momentum was exhausted; as Clausewitz said, "every pause between one success and the next gives the enemy new opportunity."[421]

---

[419] Ibid., 625.
[420] Ibid., 585–86.
[421] Clausewitz, *On War*, 626.

VI. CONCLUSION

In 1991, Major Herbert T. Holden remarked: The theories of Clausewitz are timeless because he did not analyze war from the mechanical aspects of how battles were fought between opposing generals. Instead, he analyzed warfare from the social, political, moral, and emotional perspectives as well as the tactical and strategic levels.[422]

A manuscript from Gordon R. Sullivan and LTC James M. Dubik in 1993 makes almost the same analysis.[423] More recently, Frank Ledwidge, analyzing the failure of the British military in Iraq and Afghanistan, cited Lieutenant General H.R. McMaster who emphasizes, with a view to the dead end constituted of the 1990s revolution in military affairs, that "rapid, highly mobile action has 'artificially' divorced war from its political, human and psychological dimension. ... we were behind at [the war's] outset,"[424] which is a powerful recognition of the importance and relevance of Clausewitz's thoughts today.

What made Clausewitz well-known, and still reminds us of his work, like a "subterranean river through all of modern military thought,"[425] is that we continually forget that, first, war is not a separate from a country's policy and politics has domestic as well as external facets, but is an integral part of such policy; second, that the trinity of reason, chance, and anger as well as hatred is still decisive and is the difference between defeat and victory, even more in this globalized and digitally connected world; and third, that force is not only armies and material, but also moral forces in their subtle power. This neglect of the factor of moral in the skewing of the *Schwerpünkte* of

---

[422] Major Herbert T. Holden, "The Continuing Relevance of Clausewitz: Illustrated Yesterday and Today with Application to the 1991 Persian Gulf War" (master's thesis, 1991), http://www.globalsecurity.org/military/library/report/1991/HHT.htm.

[423] Gordon R. Sullivan and Lieutenant Colonel James M. Dubrick, "Land Warfare in the 21st Century," manuscript, February 1993, cited in Dale R. Herspring, *Rumsfeld's War: The Arrogance of Power* (Lawrence: University Press of Kansas, 2008), 29–30.

[424] Cited in Ledwidge, *Losing Small Wars,* 202.

[425] Bassford, *Clausewitz in English,* 5.

reason and anger and hatred has imposed a fateful weakness on the West since 2001.

James J. Carafano remarks that, despite a generalized emphasis on technology, because senior soldiers relish an overemphasis on the Moltkean idea of a clear delineation between civilian and soldier, it is thus "unremarkable that modern military theorists made little effort to extend the principles of war much beyond the battlefield."[426] This point was that of Clausewitz in *On War*, to think in the sense of the whole and to understand the dynamics of war rather than using a checklist that may not work—as was done by Tasker Bliss in the wake of the 1918 war. His attempt to draw "lessons" from the American experience in the recent war became ineffective because they were not tailored to the conflict at hand. Carafano argues for a more holistic approach of the "new wars," and the key lies with Clausewitz. Thomas X. Hammes, in his article "the Future of Warfare,"[427] also demonstrates a relationship with Clausewitz's approach to war. Dr. Nikolas Gardner of the Air War College, in his article "Resurrecting the 'Icon'" in response to the views of Meilinger on Clausewitz, identifies the U.S. Field Manual 3–24 *Counterinsurgency* as evidence of the "impact"[428] of Clausewitz in recent military thought and credited especially David Kilcullen and John Nagl, who participated in its redaction to be the sources of influence, although not the only ones as Generals Huba Wass de Czege and Petraeus were also part of the board.

As concerns the nation-states that are still conducting wars, the trinity of chance, political effect, and anger/hatred are still relevant to the strategy and faulty choices by certain policymakers and generals of "center of gravity" led to mistakes with far-reaching consequences. Now is the time, in the view of this author, to put aside visceral reactions against Clausewitz and to start to study his work more closely;

---

[426] James J. Carafano, "Preponderance in Power: Sustaining Military Capabilities in the Twenty-First Century," in *Rethinking the Principles of War*, ed. Anthony D. McIvor (Annapolis, MD: Naval Institute Press, 2007), 227.

[427] Thomas X. Hammes, "The Future of Warfare," in *Rethinking the Principles of War*, ed. Anthony D. McIvor (Annapolis, MD: Naval Institute Press, 2007), 263–78.

[428] Nikolas Gardner, "Resurrecting the 'Icon': The Enduring Relevance of Clausewitz's *On War*," *Strategic Studies Quarterly* (Spring 2009), 128–29.

this attention has to be focused at the junction of the military and the political. Such a study is not achieved by reading it word for word. The answer is not in Jomini. Clausewitz is not a nemesis of Jomini, but an extension of the former's ideas. As Clausewitz said, "The part and the whole must always be thought of together."[429] This is the first part of the challenge—to synchronize and rebuild the "two-way bridge" of strategy between the political and military realms.

The second part of the challenge is to understand Clausewitz in the twenty-first century, to make the "parts" fit in the "whole." Although not new, communication is faster today than in Clausewitz's era. This fact challenges the strategy-makers, because they have less time than their predecessors to make sound decisions on time. Even with data collection that is faster than ever before, the "fog of war" will not disappear. In the past, the *quality* of the data was a problem. Today the *quantity* of the data represents a problem because their interpretation can lead to multiple solutions. Insofar, decision-makers need to strategize from an unbiased context of any war that may lie ahead; the solution does not lay in the quantity of data but in how those data are interpreted. Moreover, this understanding has to be done in the potential adversary's narrative and culture if planners at the strategic level want to succeed.

For Clausewitz, it was somewhat easier to understand conflicts in his time because there was no unfathomable cultural gap as might be said to operate between the think tanks of Washington, DC, and the tribal hives of the Khyber Pass. His conflicts were played between monolithic, Christian-rooted countries of Europe, although within the same structure. Today, this cultural and religious gap between the conflicting parties is wider than ever before and strategic planners need a profound understanding before committing to military actions. The violent nihilism displayed by some adversaries in the recent past defies Western nations' understanding, and Clausewitz was not confronted by a wholly similar phenomenon. However, this fact represents a new normal for a generation of fighters, and it has to be taken into account.

---

[429] Clausewitz, *On War*, 75.

In Clausewitz's time, nations' narratives were also divergent as concerned estate, dynasty, and nation and class. However, peace in 1815 settled the question, for a while, of which narrative was right. In today's conflicts, as peace is hard to attain, the narratives diverge as well. Narrative is a part of the strategy that must support the operational level of war. This narrative has to be a top-down process, coordinated with the whole of government and supported through the whole spectrum of actors, with one voice. Today, Western nations have to be realistic in their demands when going to war to secure a well-defined state of peace, understandable by all actors. Once a basic peace is secured, goodwill may build on it, incrementally. An all-or-nothing game is not possible anymore, if it ever was, in a limited-scale conflict.

Finally, those "parts" have to fit in the "whole." The "whole" as Clausewitz sees it is given for thoughts in *On War*. However, the work contains no recipe for victory. It is a foundation upon which thought unfolds and such thought can become the basis of a plan as well as action. It is a common thread that leads the strategy-makers better to understand the basics of war at the operational level and gives hints on how to solve the relationship between the "two strategies"—the political and the operational levels of war. As retired General David Petraeus remarked, "many of the concepts advanced by Clauswitz [sic] apply not just to the warfare of his day but to the warfare of our day. His thinking clearly is of enduring relevance."[430]

In the last decade, history has shown that Clausewitz's *On War* retains its relevance and contradicts its detractors, who are recycling an old canard in a new context to no good effect. The Trinitarian approach—when seen as political purpose, chance, and the political psychology of anger and hatred—applies well to violent groups of people, even without a conventional nation-state. This combination of factors in actual war, even holy war and counterinsurgency, continue to be relevant for understanding war's interaction between respective and conflicted elements that defy a mathematical formula or a business school dogma. Terrorism, as sectarian or as a nation, uses people to convey political message and to achieve goals. Thus, instead

---

[430] General David Petraeus (Ret), personal communication, May 13, 2015.

of searching for who is at fault between Jomini and Clausewitz, it is time to go back to *Art of War* and *On War* to understand their complementarity in the twenty-first-century environment, thereby bridging the gap between Phase III and Phase IV.

Classic strategic theory retains its value, despite the changing face of conflict. Those who must master the riddles and challenges of war in the past and present, to whom this study is addressed from a Swiss military perspective and from the vantage point of the U.S. Pacific slope, are ill-served by buzzwords and contemporary superficialities. The fundamental error of these buzzwords is the elevation of tactics to the level of strategy and the stripping away of the political and social from the elemental violence of conflict in all of its terrible variety. The element of anger and hatred demands its tribute today from strategists, just as Clausewitz recognized in his time.

VII. LIST OF REFERENCES

Alterman, Eric R. "Thinking Twice: The Weinberger Doctrine and the Lessons of Vietnam." *The Fletcher Forum* (Winter 1986): 95.

Arendt, Hannah. *On Violence*. New York: A Harvest Book Harcourt, 1970.

Bacevich, Andrew J. *Breach of Trust: How Americans Failed Their Soldiers and Their Country*. New York: Metropolitan Books, 2013.

Bassford, Christopher. *Clausewitz in English: The Reception of Clausewitz in Britain and America, 1815–1945*. New York: Oxford University Press, 1994.

———. "Clausewitz in America Today." In *Clausewitz Goes Global: Carl von Clausewitz in the 21st Century* [Commemorating the 50th Anniversary of the Clausewitz Society], edited by Clausewitz Gesellschaft, Reiner Pommerin, 342–56. Berlin: Carola Hartmann Miles Verlag, 2011.

Bolger, Daniel P. *Why We Lost: A General's Inside Account of the Iraq and Afghanistan Wars*. Boston: Houghton Mifflin Harcourt, 2014.

Bremer, Paul L. "Coalition Provisional Authority Order Number 2." (Accessed May 15, 2015). http://www.iraqcoalition.org/regulations/20030823_CPAORD_2_Dissolution_of_Entities_with_Annex_A.pdf.

Carafano, James J. "Preponderance in Power: Sustaining Military Capabilities in the Twenty-First Century." In *Rethinking the Principles of War*, edited by Anthony D McIvor. Annapolis, MD: Naval Institute Press, 2007.

Chairman of the Joint Chiefs of Staff. *Counterterrorism* (Joint Publication 3–26). Washington, DC: Department of Defense, October 24, 2014.

Colson, Bruno. *La Culture Stratégique Américaine*. Paris: Economica, 1993.

Connable, Ben. "Culture Warriors: Marine Corps Organizational Culture and Adaptation to Cultural Terrain." *Small Wars Journal* (February 7, 2008). http://smallwarsjournal.com/jrnl/art/culture-warriors.

Cordesman, Anthony H. and Abraham R. Wagner. *The Lessons of Modern War. Vol. IV* (Boulder, CO; London: Westview Press, 1990.

Corn, Tony. "From Mars to Minerva: Clausewitz, Liddell Hart, and the Two Western Ways of War." *Small Wars Journal* (May 21, 2011). http://smallwarsjournal.com/.

Daase, Christopher and Sebastian Schindler. "Clausewitz, Guerillakrieg und Terrorismus. Zur Aktualitat einer missvertandenen Kriegstheorie." *Politische Viertljahresschrift* 50 (2009). Doi:s11615-009-0153-2.

de Durand, Étienne. "France." In *Understanding Counterinsurgency: Doctrine, Operations, and Challenges*. Eds. Thomas Rid and Thomas Keaney. London and New York: Routledge, 2010.

deFelice, Jim. *Omar Bradley: General at War*. Washington, DC: Regnery History, 2011.

D'Este, Carlo. *Eisenhower: A Soldier's Life*. New York: Henry Holt & Co., 2002.

Dubik, James M. "Winning Battles, Losing Wars." *Army Magazine* (November 18, 2014). http://www.armymagazine.org/2014/11/18/winning-battles-losing-wars/#sthash.SPtDmfiy.dpbs%20.

Echevarria, Antulio J., II. *Clausewitz and Contemporary War*. New York: Oxford University Press, 2007.

——— and U.S. Army War College. "Fourth-Generation War and Other Myths." Carlisle Barracks, PA: Strategic Studies Institute, U.S. Army War College, 2005.

Edström, Håkan, and Dennis Gyllensporre. *Pursuing Strategy* (February 2012). http://www.palgraveconnect.com/pc/doifinder/10.1057/9780230364196.0001.

Forbes, Ian. "Future Warfare and the Principles of War." In *Rethinking the Principles of War*, ed. Anthony McIvor. Annapolis, MD: Naval Institute Press, 2005.

Freedman, Lawrence. *Strategy: A History*. New York: Oxford University Press, 2013.

Friedmann, Brett. "Creeping Death." *Military Review* (January–February 2014): 82–89.

Gardner, Nikolas. "Resurrecting the 'Icon': The Enduring Relevance of Clausewitz's *On War*." *Strategic Studies Quarterly* (Spring 2009):119-133.

Gentile, Gian. *Wrong Turn: America's Deadly Embrace of Counterinsurgency*. New York: The New Press, 2013.

GlobalSecurity.org. "Iraqi Police Service (IPS)." Last modified December 1, 2012. http://www.globalsecurity.org/intell/world/iraq/ips.htm.

Governing. "Law Enforcement Officers Per Capita for Cities, Local Departments." Table, accessed April 24, 2015, http://www.governing.com/gov-data/safety-justice/law-enforcement-police-department-employee-totals-for-cities.html.

Gordon, Michael R., and Bernard E. Trainor. *Cobra II: The Inside Story of the Invasion and Occupation of Iraq*. New York: Pantheon Books, 2006.

Gray, Colin S. "British and American Strategic Cultures." Paper presented at the *Jamestown Symposium*, March 2007, Norfolk, VA.

———. "Principles of War or Principles of Battle?" in *Rethinking the Principles of War*. Ed. McIvor, Anthony. Annapolis, MD: Naval Institute Press, 2005.

———. "Out of the Wilderness: Prime-Time for Strategic Culture." National Institute for Public Policy. Prepared Under: Advanced Strategic Planning and Analysis Support Contract with the National Institute for Public Policy, Contract No. SP0600-04-C-5982 In support of the U.S. Nuclear Strategy Forum. July 2006. https://fas.org/irp/agency/dod/dtra/stratcult-out.pdf.

Hahlweg, Werner. *Guerilla: Krieg Ohne Fronten*. Berlin: Kohlhammer, 1968.

———. "Clausewitz and Guerrilla Warfare." *Journal of Strategic Studies* 9 no. 2–3 (1986): 127–33. Doi:10.1080/01402398608437262.

Hammes, Thomas X. "The Future of Warfare." In *Rethinking the Principles of War*, edited by Anthony D McIvor. Annapolis, MD: Naval Institute Press, 2007.

Herspring, Dale R. *Rumsfeld's War: The Arrogance of Power*. Lawrence: University Press of Kansas, 2008.

Heuser, Beatrice. *The Evolution of Strategy: Thinking War from Antiquity to the Present*. New York: Cambridge University Press, 2010.

Hoffman, Frank. *Conflict in the 21st Century: The Rise of Hybrid War*. Arlington: Potomac Institute for Policy Studies, 2007. http://www.potomacinstitute.org/publications/Potomac_Hybrid_War_0108.pdf.

Holden, Herbert T. "The Continuing Relevance of Clausewitz: Illustrated Yesterday and Today with Application to the 1991 Persian Gulf War." Master's thesis, Command and Staff College, 1991. http://www.globalsecurity.org/military/library/report/1991/HHT.htm.

Howard, Michael Eliot. *War in European History*. New York: Oxford University Press, 1976.

Hugh, Edward. "Metis, Bie and Kerdos: Some Thoughts on Defeating Terrorism," *A Fistful of Euros: A European Opinion (Blog)*. Last updated March 13, 2004. http://fistfulofeuros.net/afoe/metis-bie-and-kerdos-some-thoughts-on-defeating-terrorism/.

Huntington, Samuel P. *The Soldier and the State: The Theory and Politics of Civil-military Relations*. Cambridge, MA: Belknap Press of Harvard University Press, 1957.

Independent International Commission on Kosovo. *The Kosovo Report*. New York: Oxford University Press, 2000. http://reliefweb.int/sites/reliefweb.int/files/resources/6D26FF88119644CFC1256989005CD392-thekosovoreport.pdf.

Jeffers, Paul H. *Marshall: Lessons in Leadership*. New York: Palgrave Macmillan, 2010.

Johnson, Michael W. "Clausewitz on Kosovo: A Monograph." Master's thesis, U.S. Army Command and General Staff College, School of Advanced Military Studies, 2000.

Jomini, Antoine Henri. *The Art of War*. Translated by Charles Messenger. London: Greenhill Books, 1992.

Kahin, George. *Intervention: How America Became Involved in Vietnam*. New York: Knopf, 1986.

Kaplan, Fred M. *The Insurgents: David Petraeus and the Plot to Change the American Way of War*. New York: Simon & Schuster, 2013.

Kilcullen, David. *Out of the Mountains: The Coming Age of the Urban Guerrilla*. New York: Oxford University Press, 2013.

Kinross, Stuart. *Clausewitz and America: Strategic Thought and Practice from Vietnam to Iraq*. London: Routledge, 2008.

Leonhard, Robert R. *The Principles of War for the Information Age*. Novato, CA: Presidio Press, 2000.

Lisagor, Philip. "Don't Bring Back the Powell Doctrine." *Cicero Magazine*, February 11, 2015. http://ciceromagazine.com/opinion/dont-bring-back-the-powell-doctrine/.

Marlantes, Karl. *What It Is Like to Go to War*. New York: Atlantic Monthly Press, 2011.

Maslow, Abraham H. "A Theory of Human Motivation." *Psychological Review* 50, 370–96 (1943). http://psychclassics.yorku.ca/Maslow/motivation.htm.

McGrath, John J. "The Other End of the Spear: The Tooth-to-Tail Ratio (T3R) in Modern Military Operations." In *The Long War Series Occasional Paper 23. Combat Studies*. Fort Leavenworth, KS: Institute Press, 2007.

McIvor, Anthony. *Rethinking the Principles of War*. Annapolis, MD: Naval Institute Press, 2005.

Melton, Stephen L. *The Clausewitz Delusion: How the American Army Screwed Up the War in Iraq and Afghanistan*. Minneapolis: Zenith Press, 2009.

Münkler, Herfried. *Les Guerres Nouvelles*. Translated by Catherine Obétais. Paris: Alvik Éditions, 2003.

Nagl, John A. *Learning to Eat Soup with a Knife: Counterinsurgency Lessons from Malaya and Vietnam*. University of Chicago Press, 2005.

National Commission on Terrorist Attacks upon the United States. *The Foundation of the New Terrorism* (accessed on May 15, 2015). http://www.9-11commission.gov/report/911Report_Ch2.htm.

North Atlantic Treaty Organisation (NATO). *The Alliance's New Strategic Concept*. Brussels: NATO, November 8, 1991. http://www.nato.int/cps/en/natolive/official_texts_23847.htm.

———. *The Alliance's New Strategic Concept.* Brussels: NATO, April 24, 1999. http://www.nato.int/cps/en/natohq/official_texts_27433.htm.

———. *The Alliance's New Strategic Concept.* Brussels: NATO, November 19, 2010. http://www.nato.int/cps/en/natohq/official_texts_68580.htm.

———. *The Committee of Three.* 1956. http://www.nato.int/archives/committee_of_three/CT.pdf.

———. "Future Tasks of the Alliance—'Harmel Report.'" Last updated November 14, 2011. http://www.nato.int/cps/en/natolive/80830.htm.

———. *NATO Handbook.* Brussels: Public Diplomacy Division, 2006. http://www.nato.int/docu/handbook/2006/hb-en-2006.pdf.

———. *The North Atlantic Treaty.* Washington, DC: April 4, 1949. http://www.nato.int/cps/en/natolive/official_texts_17120.htm.

Osgood, Robert Endicott. *Limited War: The Challenge to American Strategy.* Chicago, IL: University of Chicago Press, 1957.

Paret, Peter. *Clausewitz and the State: The Man, His Theories, and His Times.* Princeton, NJ: Princeton University Press, 2007.

———, Gordon Alexander Craig, and Felix Gilbert. *Makers of Modern Strategy: From Machiavelli to the Nuclear Age.* Princeton, NJ: Princeton University Press, 1986

Patry, Jean-Jacques, and Nicole Vilboux. "Contre-Insurrection et « Nouvelles » Doctrines Militaires: L'adieu aux Illusions!" *Fondation pour la Recherche Stratégique.* Note 02/12, 10 (January 2012). http://www.isn.ethz.ch/Digital-Library/Publications/Detail/?lng=en&id=136512.

Pedlow, Gregory W, ed. *NATO Strategy Documents 1949–1969.* Mons, Belgium: Supreme Headquarters Allied Powers Europe, 1997. http://www.nato.int/archives/strategy.htm.

Pitt, William Rivers, and Scott Ritter. *War on Iraq: What Team Bush Doesn't Want You to Know.* New York: Context Books, 2002.

Porch, Douglas. *Counterinsurgency: Exposing the Myths of the New Way of War.* New York: Cambridge University Press, 2013.

Prescott, Jody M. "The Development of NATO EBAO Doctrine: Clausewitz's Theories and the Role of Law in an Evolving Approach to Operations." *Penn State International Law Review* 27, no 1 (Summer 2008).

President of the United States. "National Strategy for Counterterrorism." Washington, D.C.: The White House, June 28, 2011, https://www.whitehouse.gov/sites/default/files/counterterrorism_strategy.pdf.

Rothe, Andreas Herberg. "A Prussian in the United States." *Europäische Sicherheit* (October 2003). http://www.clausewitz.com/readings/Herberg-Rothe/CWZintheUSA.htm.

Schmitt, Carl. *The Concept of the Political.* Chicago: The University of Chicago Press, 2007.

Simpson, Emile. *War from the Ground Up: Twenty-First Century Combat as Politics.* New York: Oxford University Press, 2013.

Summers, Harry G. *On Strategy: The Vietnam War in Context* (Carlisle Barracks, PA : Washington, D.C.: Strategic Studies Institute, U.S. Army War College, 1981).

Stoker, Donald J. *Clausewitz: His Life and Work.* New York: Oxford University Press, 2014.

Stoler, Mark A. *Allies and Adversaries: The Joint Chiefs of Staff, the Grand Alliance, and U.S. Strategy in World War II.* Chapel Hill: University of North Carolina Press, 2000.

Strachan, Hew. *The Direction of War: Contemporary Strategy in Historical Perspective.* New York: Cambridge University Press, 2013.

Sullivan, Gordon R., and James M. Dubrick. "Land Warfare in the 21st Century." Manuscript, February 1993. Cited in Dale R. Herspring, *Rumsfeld's War: the Arrogance of Power.* Lawrence: University Press of Kansas, 2008.

Thomas, Ian Q. R. *The Promise of Alliance: NATO and the Political Imagination.* Lanham, MA: Rowman and Littlefield, 1997.

Tooke, Lamar, and Ralph Allen. "Strategic Intuition and the Art of War." *Military Review* LXXV, no. 2 (March–April 2994): 10–19.

http://cgsc.contentdm.oclc.org/cdm/ref/collection/p124201coll1/id/443.

Treisman, Daniel. "Clausewitz in Afghanistan." University of California, Los Angeles. http://www.sscnet.ucla.edu/polisci/faculty/treisman/Papers/clause.pdf.

Tremblay, Éric, and Bill Bentley. "Canada's Strategic Culture: Grand Strategy and the Utility of Force." *Canadian Military Journal* 15, no. 3 (2015). http://www.journal.forces.gc.ca/vol15/no3/page5-eng.asp.

Thucydides, Rex Warner, and M. I. Finley. *History of the Peloponnesian War*. New York, NY: Penguin Books, 1972.

Ullman, Harlan K., and James P. Wade. "Shock and Awe: Achieving Rapid Dominance." *NDU Pressbook*. Washington, DC: National Defense University Center for Advanced Concepts and Technology (December 1996). http://www.au.af.mil/au/awc/awcgate/ndu/shocknawe/ch2.html.

U.S. Joint Chiefs of Staff. *Joint Operation Planning*. Washington, DC: Joint Chiefs of Staff, 2011.

van Creveld, Martin. *The Transformation of War*. New York: The Free Press, 1991.

von Clausewitz, Carl. *On War*. Edited and translated by Michael Howard and Peter Paret. Princeton, NJ: Princeton University Press, 1984.

Wagner, Henry Halleck. *Elements of Military Art and Science; or, Course of Instruction in Strategy, Fortification, Tactics of Battles, &c.; Embracing the Duties of Staff, Infantry, Cavalry, Artillery, and Engineers. Adapted to the Use of Volunteers and Militia*. New York: D. Appleton & Co., 1846. https://archive.org/details/elementsofmilita00hall.

Wigley, Russell F. *The American Way of War: A History of United States Military Strategy and Policy*. Bloomington: Indiana University Press, 1977.

Willis, Steve. "Clausewitz and Corbett Are Now Too Much." Center for International Maritime Security (March 5, 2015). http://cimsec.org/clausewitz-corbett-now-much/15338.

World Bank. Data: Iraq. Accessed April 24, 2015. http://data.worldbank.org/country/iraq.

Yost, David S. *NATO's Balancing Act*. Washington, DC: United States Institute of Peace Press, 2014.

———. *NATO Transformed: The Alliance's New Roles in International Security*. Washington, DC: United States Institute of Peace Press, 1998.

Zinni, Tony, and Tony Koltz. *Before the First Shots Are Fired: How America Can Win or Lose Off the Battlefield*. New York: Palgrave MacMillan, 2014.

Carola Hartmann Miles-Verlag

Politik, Gesellschaft, Militär

Uwe Hartmann, *Innere Führung. Erfolge und Defizite der Führungsphilosophie für die Bundeswehr*, Berlin 2007.

Hans Joachim Reeb, *Sicherheitskultur als kommunikative und pädagogische Herausforderung – Der Umgang in Politik, Medien und Gesellschaft*, Berlin 2011.

Hans-Christian Beck, Christian Singer (Hrsg.), *Entscheiden – Führen – Verantworten. Soldatsein im 21. Jahrhundert*, Berlin 2011.

Eberhard Birk, Winfried Heinemann, Sven Lange (Hrsg.), *Tradition für die Bundeswehr. Neue Aspekte einer alten Debatte*, Berlin 2012.

Angelika Dörfler-Dierken, *Führung in der Bundeswehr*, Berlin 2013.

Cornelia Fedtke, Kai-Uwe Hellmann, Jan Hörmann, *Migration und Militär. Zur Integration deutscher Soldaten mit Migrationshintergrund in der Bundeswehr*, Berlin 2013.

Wolf Graf von Baudissin, *Grundwert Frieden in Politik – Strategie – Führung von Streitkräften*, hrsg. von Claus von Rosen, Berlin 2014.

Wolf Graf von Baudissin, *Der Widerstand. „… um nie wieder in die ausweglose Lage zu geraten…"*, hrsg. von Claus von Rosen, Berlin 2014.

Marcel Bohnert, Lukas J. Reitstetter (Hrsg.), *Armee im Aufbruch. Zur Gedankenwelt junger Offiziere in den Kampftruppen der Bundeswehr*, Berlin 2014.

Arjan Kozica, Kai Prüter, Hannes Wendroth (Hrsg.), *Unternehmen Bundeswehr? Theorie und Praxis (militärischer) Führung*, Berlin 2014.

Angelika Dörfler-Dierken, Robert Kramer, *Innere Führung in Zahlen. Streitkräftebefragung 2013*, Berlin 2014.

Eberhard Birk, Heiner Möllers (Hrsg.), *Luftwaffe und Luftkrieg*, Berlin 2015.

Phil C. Langer, Gerhard Kümmel (Hrsg.), *„Wir sind Bundeswehr." Wie viel Vielfalt benötigen/vertragen die Streitkräfte?*, Berlin 2015.

Dirk Freudenberg, *Counterinsurgency. Aufstandsbekämpfung als Phase zur Überwindung schwacher Staatlichkeit und zur Etablierung des Aufbaus einer stabilen Nachkriegsordnung?*, Berlin 2016.

Jahrbuch Innere Führung

Uwe Hartmann, Claus von Rosen, Christian Walther (Hrsg.), *Jahrbuch Innere Führung 2009. Die Rückkehr des Soldatischen,* Eschede 2009.

Helmut R. Hammerich, Uwe Hartmann, Claus von Rosen (Hrsg.), *Jahrbuch Innere Führung 2010. Die Grenzen des Militärischen* lin 2010.

Uwe Hartmann, Claus von Rosen, Christian Walther (Hrsg.), *Jahrbuch Innere Führung 2011. Ethik als geistige Rüstung für Soldaten,* Berlin 2011.

Uwe Hartmann, Claus von Rosen, Christian Walther (Hrsg.), *Jahrbuch Innere Führung 2012. Der Soldatenberuf zwischen gesellschaftlicher Integration und suis generis-Ansprüchen,* Berlin 2012.

Uwe Hartmann, Claus von Rosen (Hrsg.), *Jahrbuch Innere Führung 2013. Wissenschaften und ihre Relevanz für die Bundeswehr als Armee im Einsatz,* Berlin 2013.

Uwe Hartmann, Claus von Rosen (Hrsg.), *Jahrbuch Innere Führung 2014. Drohnen, Roboter und Cyborgs – Der Soldat im Angesicht neuer Militärtechnologien,* Berlin 2014.

Uwe Hartmann, Claus von Rosen (Hrsg.), *Jahrbuch Innere Führung 2015. Neue Denkwege angesichts der Gleichzeitigkeit unterschiedlicher Krisen, Konflikte und Kriege,* Berlin 2015.

Einsatzerfahrungen

Kay Kuhlen, *Um des lieben Friedens willen. Als Peacekeeper im Kosovo,* Eschede 2009.

Sascha Brinkmann, Joachim Hoppe (Hrsg.), *Generation Einsatz, Fallschirmjäger berichten ihre Erfahrungen aus Afghanistan,* Berlin 2010.

Artur Schwitalla, *Afghanistan, jetzt weiß ich erst… Gedanken aus meiner Zeit als Kommandeur des Provincial Reconstruction Team FEYZABAD,* Berlin 2010.

Uwe Hartmann, *War without Fighting? The Reintegration of Former Combatants in Afghanistan seen through the Lens of Strategic Thought,* Berlin 2014.

Rainer Buske, *KUNDUZ. Ein Erlebnisbericht über einen militärischen Einsatz der Bundeswehr in AFGHANISTAN im Jahre 2008,* Berlin 2015.

Standpunkte und Orientierungen

Daniel Giese, *Militärische Führung im Internetzeitalter – Die Bedeutung von Strategischer Kommunikation und Social Media für Entscheidungsprozesse, Organisationsstrukturen und Führerausbildung in der Bundeswehr,* Berlin 2014.

Dirk Freudenberg, *Auftragstaktik und Innere Führung. Feststellungen und Anmerkungen zur Frage nach Bedeutung und Verhältnis des inneren Gefüges und der Auftragstaktik unter den Bedingungen des Einsatzes der Deutschen Bundeswehr,* Berlin 2014.

Uwe Hartmann (Hrsg.), *Lernen von Afghanistan. Innovative Mittel und Wege für Auslandseinsätze,* Berlin 2015.

Fouzieh Melanie Alamir, *Vernetzte Sicherheit – Quo Vadis?,* Berlin 2015.

Hartmut von Schubert, *Integrative Militärethik. Ethische Urteilsbildung in der militärischen Führung,* Berlin 2015.

Uwe Hartmann, *Hybrider Krieg als neue Bedrohung von Freiheit und Frieden. Zur Relevanz der Inneren Führung in Politik, Gesellschaft und Streitkräften,* Berlin 2015.

Klaus Beckmann, *Treue.Bürgermut.Ungehorsam. Anstöße zur Führungskultur und zum beruflichen Selbstverständnis in der Bundeswehr,* Berlin 2015.

Militärgeschichte

Peter Heinze, *Bundeswehr „erobert" Deutschlands Osten,* Berlin 2010.

Dieter E. Kilian, *Adenauers vergessener Retter – Major Fritz Schliebusch,* Berlin 2011.

Ingo Pfeiffer, *Gegner wider Willen. Konfrontation von Volksmarine und Bundesmarine auf See,* Berlin 2012.

Dieter E. Kilian, *Kai-Uwe von Hassel und seine Familie. Zwischen Ostsee und Ostafrika. Militär-biographisches Mosaik,* Berlin 2013.

Peter Heinze, *Berliner Militärgeschichten,* Berlin 2013.

Ingo Pfeiffer, *Seestreitkräfte der DDR,* Berlin 2014.

Ulrich C. Kleyser, *Lazare Carnot. "Le Grand Carnot". Ein Charakterbild*, Berlin 2016.

Monterey Studies

Uwe Hartmann, *Carl von Clausewitz and the Making of Modern Strategy*, Potsdam 2002.

Zeljko Cepanec, *Croatia and NATO. The Stony Road to Me* Potsdam 2002.

Ekkehard Stemmer, *Demography and European Armed Force.* 2006.

Sven Lange, *Revolt against the West. A Comparison of the Curren Terror with the Boxer Rebellion in 1900-01,* Berlin 2007.

Klaus M. Brust, *Culture and the Transformation of the Bundeswehr,* Berlin 2007.

Donald Abenheim, *Soldier and Politics Transformed,* Berlin 2007.

Michael Stolzke, *The Conflict Aftermath. A Chance for Democracy: Norm Diffusion in Post-Conflict Peace Building,* Berlin 2007.

Frank Reimers, *Security Culture in Times of War. How did the Balkan War affect the Security Cultures in Germany and the United States?,* Berlin 2007.

Michael G. Lux, *Innere Führung – A Superior Concept of Leadership?,* Berlin 2009.

Marc A. Walther, *HAMAS between Violence and Pragmatism,* Berlin 2010.

Frank Hagemann, *Strategy Making in the European Union,* Berlin 2010.

Ralf Hammerstein, *Deliberalization in Jordan: the Roles of Islamists and U.S.-EU Assistance in stalled Democratization,* Berlin 2011.

Jochen Wittmann, *Auftragstaktik,* Berlin 2012.

Michael Hanisch, *On German Foreign und Security Policy. Determinants of German Military Engagement in Africa since 2011,* Berlin 2015.